INNER HEALING

Deliverance or Deception?

DON MATZAT

HARVEST HOUSE PUBLISHERS
Eugene, Oregon 97402

INNER HEALING

Copyright © 1987 by Harvest House Publishers
Eugene, Oregon 97402

Library of Congress Catalog Card Number 86-062977
ISBN 0-89081-584-4

CONTENTS

ACKNOWLEDGMENTS

Any person who has undertaken a research task of this nature realizes the consuming nature of the work. Therefore, thanks to my wife, Dianne; to Phil, Cindy, Sue, and Dan for releasing me to the task and not complaining too strongly about my absence from family matters over the past months.

A Special Thanks . . .

To the people at Resurrection Lutheran, especially to my associate Larry McReynold, to my secretary Doris Ulicny, and to Tom McNeely, the president of our congregation, for filling the gap and recognizing the importance of the task.

To Dr. Don Miles, former Deputy Commissioner of Mental Health for the State of New York, for his encouragement and valuable expertise in matters of psychology.

To Dr. Dave Benke, my golf partner, for being willing to sacrifice a few strokes by discussing theology and psychology from tee to green.

To my good friend Pastor Rod Lensch for his insights and practical advice: "If you are going to undertake the work, be sure you have the grace to do it."

To inner-healing teachers John and Paula Sandford for their valuable correspondence which underlined the serious nature of this work. While their prophetic warnings and explanations were not received, they were remembered.

Finally, to our gracious God, who provided all things necessary for life and salvation in Christ Jesus and offered such benefits in His sufficient Word. "Grant us grace, O Lord, to meet You where You have promised to be found."

INTRODUCTION

This book presents a critical evaluation of the teaching and ministry known as inner healing, soul healing, or the healing of memories. My purpose in writing this book is threefold: to provide information about the questionable concepts from the field of psychology that undergird inner healing; to raise questions regarding the potential problems and confusion created in the merging of these concepts into the body of Christian teaching; and to present a biblical alternative to inner healing.

With the exception of the last few chapters, in which I share with you that biblical alternative, I did not "enjoy" researching and writing this book, for it is a critical evaluation of a teaching that is being promoted within the body of Christ by well-intentioned Christian teachers. I do not enjoy criticizing brothers and sisters in Christ Jesus by scrutinizing what they teach. If I did, I would need to examine my own heart and be reminded that "love does not rejoice in the wrong." I offer this reminder to you the reader.

Those who teach and promote the ministry of inner healing will probably criticize this book and view it as the cause of division and controversy within the body of Christ. But on the other hand, I believe that a great deal of the confusion and controversy surrounding the inner-healing ministry could have been avoided if the inner-healing teachers would have openly shared the sources behind their teaching.

While the authors who write the books advocating the inner-healing ministry clearly indicate that they use concepts from the field of psychology and that they appreciate the insights gained from psychology, they do not come clean and reveal their specific sources. Why is this? Are the inner-healing teachers afraid that if the body of Christ knew the sources of their teaching, the teaching itself would be rejected? If they had initially been forthright in revealing the sources, and if they also had provided an acceptable rationale for the use of concepts drawn from the field of psychology as a foundation for a Christian ministry offering a healing spiritual experience, the months of research that went into the writing of this book would not have been necessary. Christians themselves, on the basis of the honest, open information provided by the inner-healing teachers themselves, could have made up their own minds as to the validity of the inner-healing ministry within the body of Christ.

If God's people want to understand the basis of inner healing they are forced to plow through the theories governing human behavior proposed within the field of psychology. Not many within the body of Christ have the desire or perhaps even ability to understand the variety of ideas which make up psychology. We cannot discuss inner healing on the basis of Matthew, Mark, Luke, John, Romans, or Ephesians. Rather, we are forced to understand Freud, Jung, Missildine, Berne, Rank, and the like.

Researching the inner-healing technique is not an easy task. In addition to the fact that sources are often hidden, it is very difficult to discover clear definitions in the writings of the inner-healing authors. It is generally known, for example, that the technique of visualization is used by inner healers. They all refer to the method, speaking of "visualization prayer," "faith-imagination therapy," "consecrated and committed imagination," or "active imagination." Why? What is the purpose of using imagination? Where did the idea originate? Is it based upon Scripture? If not, which school of psychology utilizes visualization as a therapeutic technique? These questions often go unanswered. Clear definition is often lost in verbal piety and the sharing of personal testimonies.

I have attempted to do as honest a job as possible of research and evaluation of the various psychological concepts undergirding inner healing. I have sought to explain these concepts, many of them quite complex, in understandable terminology. I am not writing for the trained counselor or theologian, but for the average Christian who is seeking some insight into the existing problems surrounding the inner-healing ministry. I am beginning with the assumption that those who are reading this book have had some exposure to the inner-healing ministry but have had minimal exposure to the ideas presented within the various schools of psychology. My purpose is not to destroy the inner-healing movement as such, but rather to point out what is behind inner healing. If such exposure does bring harm to the inner-healing movement, so be it. I do not believe that any legitimate movement of God within the church is damaged by bringing it into the light of public scrutiny. Sincere Christian teachers should welcome and desire the light of scrutiny, since their major motivation is the welfare of God's people.

I do not wish to build a reputation on the practice of criticizing the teachings of other people. I hope that you will find within these pages helpful insight which is drawn from the Word of God and which will help you to live and walk in Christ Jesus. It is also my fervent prayer that, as a result of the reading of this book, you will commit yourself to remaining securely within biblical boundaries in your pursuit of truth and life-changing experience. To this end, may God be praised!

—Donald G. Matzat
March 1987

An Intriguing Debate

1

An Intriguing Debate

The book *The Seduction of Christianity*, by Dave Hunt and T.A. McMahon, has created a major stir within a rather large segment of the Christian church, especially within the charismatic movement. By citing the works of many popular Bible teachers and charismatic pastors and leaders, the authors of *Seduction* documented what they claimed to be a major deception infiltrating the ranks of the church. This deception, according to Hunt and McMahon, is in part a manifestation of the New Age movement and may in fact be the great deception and falling away which the Bible predicts will occur prior to the culmination of this age.[1]

Numerous leaders within the charismatic movement vehemently denied the claims of Hunt and McMahon and rushed to the defense of those whose teachings had been critically examined by the authors. After reading both *The Seduction of Christianity* and the reviews of various charismatic leaders (some of whom I knew personally), my curiosity was aroused. How could it be, I questioned, that Hunt and McMahon could claim that certain erroneous concepts and even occult heresies were being taught by specific individuals within the church and then go on to extensively document those claims, while Christian leaders such as Jamie Buckingham, Dennis Bennett, John Loren Sandford, and others could adamantly deny that the claims were true? Both parties in this debate could not be right. Either Hunt and McMahon were immoral sensationalists, or the charismatic leaders denying the truth of the claims and the validity of the research contained in *The Seduction of Christianity* were guilty of producing a cover-up, or else there was some middle position that had to be discovered. To say the least, the conflict produced a very intriguing situation.

WHAT'S THE ANSWER?

I was particularly shocked by the accusation made by the authors of *Seduction* that the late Agnes Sanford, one of the early teachers and major influences within the charismatic movement, based her controversial concept of inner healing upon the psychological theories of Carl Jung.[2] They also pointed out that the technique of visualization employed in the inner-healing methodology was an occult technique which had no place within the body of Christ. They referred to the technique as "sorcery." Could such an accusation be true?

Having been a part of the charismatic movement for over 15 years, I deeply respected and admired many of the charismatic leaders who taught inner healing. Personally, I had never really embraced the inner-healing ministry and knew very little about it. But could it possibly be true that men such as Dennis Bennett, Francis MacNutt, or Jamie Buckingham were in fact deceived and seduced? I found that hard to believe. I had met Dennis Bennett, and we had corresponded on a few occasions. His books *Nine O'clock in the Morning* and *The Holy Spirit and You* were textbooks I had used with members of my congregation in Michigan. I sat next to Francis MacNutt during one of the evening sessions at a conference on the Holy Spirit in Minneapolis. Charismatics are deeply indebted to Jamie Buckingham for defining the things of God in meaningful terminology. To claim that such men are seduced and deceived was difficult to accept.

In defending the ministry of inner healing, John Loren Sandford, a disciple of Agnes Sanford and a proponent of the inner-healing methodology, strongly denied the Jungian/occult accusation. He stated in his November 1985 *Elijah House* newsletter that Agnes Sanford actually warned her hearers not to get caught up in psychology. Sandford also defended the visualization technique, claiming that the Holy Spirit provided visions within the inner-healing ministry which Hunt and McMahon were confusing with visualization.

The response of Sandford to the accusations of Hunt and McMahon produced a "black-and-white" impasse. Since the accusation and the denial were so polarized, it logically followed that somebody had to be right and somebody had to be wrong. I decided to try to discover the answer to these questions: *Did Agnes Sanford base her inner-healing technique upon Jungian psychology or was she actually against Jungianism? Is the technique of visualization employed within inner healing occult in nature? Was it possible that inner-healing teachers were dabbling in occultism?*

UNCLEAR ISSUES AND ANSWERS

In assessing the conflict that has arisen over the claims and counterclaims precipitated by *The Seduction of Christianity*, I do not believe that the issues have been clearly explained. While the authors raised some red flags, we have not yet seen a clear and sufficiently detailed explanation of the issues to enable God's people to understand what is wrong, if anything, with the inner-healing method.

For example, Hunt and McMahon accurately pointed out that Agnes Sanford undergirded her inner-healing methods with the Jungian concept of the *collective unconscious*. But what does that mean? What is the collective unconscious? What is the basis for this Jungian theory? What is the problem involved with the acceptance of this theory? Will the theory fit into the biblical perspective? These subjects were not covered in *Seduction*. In order for people to understand the problem and form an opinion, they first need to be able to understand the concepts that are allegedly erroneous. I think it is only fair to point out that the authors of *Seduction* covered such a large body of material that to have provided detailed explanations on every issue would have produced an impractically massive volume. I am dealing with the specific issue of inner healing. My purpose is to provide greater detail on this single issue, and not to point out the existence of a massive seduction involving many areas and issues.

I do not believe that the advocates of inner healing, in responding to the questions raised by Hunt and McMahon, have cooperated in shedding much light on the problem. In fact, I believe that their responses have clouded the issues by refusing to honestly deal with them. For example, one of the major issues raised in *Seduction* regarding the inner-healing technique is the claim by the Roman Catholic practitioners of inner healing that the visualization of the Virgin Mary is as effective for the healing of past hurts as is the visualization of Jesus.[3] In the many reviews and magazine articles defending the inner-healing technique, and also in the book *The Church Divided* (released by Bridge Publishing as a response to *Seduction*), this issue was never addressed. Why not?

In addition, the arguments used by the inner-healing teachers in debating the accusations raised by Hunt and McMahon are very questionable and avoid the real issues. For example, in *Seduction* the question was raised about using the psychological theory of the unconscious mind (a theory first popularized by Sigmund Freud) as an undergirding basis for spiritual experience. The authors pointed out that the concept of the unconscious is not found in the Bible. Inner-healing advocate Robert Wise responded by stating that the objection is as absurd as trying to find a biblical text to support the use of cars or electric lights.[4]

But this argument is highly irrational. I have never heard anyone claim that God is able to be discovered in cars or in electric lights, yet such claims have been made by those who have probed the unconscious mind. To compare the use of automobiles and electric lights with the inner-healing teachers' use of the theory of the unconscious mind seems to be nothing more than a straw-man technique employed to divert attention away from the real issues.

THE REAL ISSUE

What is the real issue? Before answering this question, let us consider questions which are *not* the real issue.

There are many schools of psychology, each offering its own interpretation of human behavior. There are few theories that

If a single theory is accepted, must not the underlying assumptions which led to the development of that theory also be accepted? Can one accept, for example, Einstein's theory of relativity but reject the existence of energy? Of course not.

We have a great deal of work to do and many questions to answer. Let us begin by exploring the nature and purpose of the inner-healing teaching and technique.

The Key to Sanctification?

2

The Key to Sanctification?

I believe that much of the charismatic movement has been a source of blessing to the church of Jesus Christ. In spite of the many problems and conflicts that have been associated with the movement, the fact remains that literally millions of people the world over have been positively impacted by the emphasis upon the Holy Spirit and His gifts. Many lives have been changed, many families brought together, many ministries revitalized, many churches renewed. Who can number the people in both Catholic and Protestant church bodies who have been delivered from bondage to dead traditions and brought into a new, glorious relationship with the living Lord Jesus Christ through the experience of the Holy Spirit? I count myself among those people whose lives have been changed by the charismatic renewal.

In spite of the favorable results that history will undoubtedly attribute to the charismatic renewal in terms of changed lives and renewed churches, the renewal has not fulfilled the high expectations that have been held for it. The sincere desire of those occupying positions of pastoral leadership within the renewal has been to see the maturity of the body of Christ, the equipping of the bride for the coming of the Bridegroom, and the establishment of committed bodies of Christians who are manifesting forth the power and reality of the living Christ. Such vision has come far short of fulfillment. Many individuals within the charismatic-renewal movement desire new truth, new revelation, a "new wave," or a fresh outpouring of the Holy Spirit to complete what is still lacking.

THE LACK OF MATURITY

The major shortcoming visible within the charismatic renewal, at least in the eyes of those who occupy positions of leadership, has been the lack of sanctification, stability, and maturity in the lives of those who have otherwise experienced the reality of the movement. While many have entered into the charismatic dimension through the renewal experience, not all have become genuinely committed, matured, stabilized, useful members of the body of Christ. Behavior problems which plagued Christians prior to their renewal experience do not seem to go away. In many cases, changed lives resulting from the renewal experience have been temporary. The old problems, hang-ups, and habits have a way of sticking up their ugly heads again and again. Many people within the renewal seemingly live on a spiritual roller coaster. Unable to shake the problems of the sinful flesh, their experience is up one day and down the next. Immorality, divorce, anger, broken relationships, lack of forgiveness, worry, and fear are still being named among charismatics, hindering the movement from accomplishing the goal of producing maturity, stability, and committed relationships among the people of God. It is true that many "free fellowships" comprised of charismatics who have left their institutional involvements have sprung up around the country, offering the hope of fulfillment for the charismatic vision. Yet the existence of such fellowships is often short-lived because it is readily splintered by the failure of God's people to relate together in unity. This has produced much disillusionment and disappointment among charismatics.

This "charismatic problem" led a committed group of leaders in the renewal movement to initiate the discipleship/shepherding movement back in the middle seventies. Out of a sincere desire to see the development of maturity within the body of Christ, popular leaders within the renewal encouraged charismatics to come under the authority of a "shepherd" who would help bring discipline into the life of the "disciple," thereby producing stable maturity. A "Shepherding Conference" in Kansas City in 1975 brought together thousands of discipleship advocates from around the country, proclaiming a new day in the kingdom. While many respected leaders saw this movement as the solution to the lack of maturity problem, time demonstrated otherwise. The lack of a clear biblical foundation for the movement, the excesses in the application of authority, the bondage of legalism, and the failure of the leaders themselves to maintain covenanted, submitted relationships among themselves caused the effort to produce little fruit and further disillusionment.

THE INNER-HEALING SOLUTION

The ministry of inner healing or soul healing is another attempt to solve the problem and bring charismatics into maturity and stability. The inner-healing movement offers its own analysis of the charismatic dilemma. An interesting article on the subject of inner healing published in a recent issue of *Charisma* magazine speaks of the growing popularity of the inner-healing movement. The article suggested that what is being diagnosed today as the need for inner healing would have probably been viewed ten years ago as the need for deliverance from demons.[1] According to inner-healing teachers, the problem is not the lack of spiritual authority or the influence of demons, but that *the hidden problems, sins, and traumas of the past, inflicted primarily during childhood, continue to plague the Christian in the present, hindering the development of sanctification, maturity, and stability.* Inner-healing teachers desire to set people free from the chains to the past.

It is generally agreed that the founder of the inner-healing ministry was the late Agnes Sanford. Together with her husband, Ted, an Episcopal priest, Mrs. Sanford founded the Schools of Pastoral Care, where inner healing was taught and offered as early as the late fifties and early sixties. Many of the popular inner-healing teachers of today learned the technique from Agnes Sanford and regard her as the founder of the movement.

Describing the negative experiences and traumas of the past which become the objects of inner healing, or what she called "the healing of memories," Agnes Sanford wrote:

What can we do about the chains of time—the burdens put upon our souls when we were too little to be responsible? If the sorrows of a child can weigh still upon the soul of a grown person and if the fears of a child transfer themselves into irrational phobias in the mind of a grown person, then what hope is there for anyone, our personalities being so intricately involved with time and Time?[2]

Describing her initial involvement with the method for the healing of her own memories, Mrs. Sanford writes:

Then I sent my mind back in time and tried to remember the eighth year of my life and to review it, so that God through the subconscious mind could put His finger on a sore spot and say "That is it." . . . I went back in the memories and found that little child, and, playing a game in the imagination, I told her that she was loved and comforted and that she would also be healed. Opening thus a door into the past, I took Jesus with me and led Him to her that He might heal her with His love.[3]

According to the inner-healing teachers, the traumas and burdens of the past continue to plague the Christian in the present. Before victory and sanctification can be realized, these hurts must be healed.

LOCATING THE PROBLEM

According to the inner-healing teachers, the part of the "soul" which is the object of "soul healing" or the "inner" element in "inner healing" (or the location of the memories in "the healing of memories") is the *unconscious or the subconscious mind*. Popular charismatic teacher Dr. Paul Yonggi Cho of Korea, who Pastors the world's largest congregation, is not specifically an inner-healing teacher, but in his teaching on "the fourth dimension" he uses the concept of the unconscious mind as being a source of supernatural power. In defining the hidden motivation arising from the unconscious which hinders sanctification, Dr. Cho provides an excellent definition of inner healing:

> What is referred to as the subconscious is really the unconscious mind. The unconscious mind is the motivational force that causes men to act or to behave without conscious perception. . . . If our actions and accomplishments result from a motivating force that is beyond our conscious perception, then should not the Holy Spirit choose to work within this realm in order to sanctify it and cause it to motivate us to do God's will?[4]

The basic premise of inner healing is that the unconscious mind must be sanctified, transformed, and healed in order for sanctification and Christian maturity to take place. Referring to the unconscious mind, Agnes Sanford states, ". . . if I am to be a whole person, this area of emanation or of interpenetration must also be healed."[5] Dennis and Rita Bennett teach that the most serious blocks to the free flow of spiritual life are found within the subconscious. They suggest that Jesus, according to the promise in Revelation 3:20, is knocking on the door of the subconscious, desiring to heal our hurting memories and damaged emotions.[6] Because the concept of the unconscious mind is a controversial subject, as we will clearly discover in later chapters, some of the inner-healing teachers refrain from using the term. John and Paula Sandford, for example, speak of the *deep mind and heart of our spirit*.[7] This is a difficult definition to understand. It is not clear whether they are equating the unconscious mind with the "heart" or the "spirit."

VICTIMS OF THE PAST

The past hurts and traumas located within the unconscious mind which become the object of inner healing are problems

which are not of our own making. The ministry of inner healing is
directed at "victims of the past." Ruth Carter Stapleton points
out:

> As we respond to prayer by imagining Jesus moving
> back into our lives, we picture the little child within us
> who hurts, who was rejected, who failed to receive
> healthy love, who was neglected by the parents' failure
> to give corrective discipline in love, who wasn't under-
> stood. That little child within each of us must harken to
> the healing love of Jesus.[8]

According to Rita Bennett, the hurts of the past are "rocks in
our river." She points out that soul healing is mainly concerned
with the rocks that have been dropped into our stream of life by
other people.[9]

According to inner-healing teachers, we are the victims of our
past. Because of what others have inflicted upon us in terms of
traumatic experiences, we are unable to develop spiritual maturity and stability. When it comes to overcoming personal problems, the biblical understanding of repentance is impossible, not
only because we are "unconscious" of the hurts of the past but
also because *we are not responsible* for the hurts of the past.

THE KEY TO SANCTIFICATION?

The motives of those who advocate the inner-healing ministry
are sincere. Similar to the attitude of the "discipleship teachers,"
the inner-healing teachers believe that they have the answer to the
charismatic dilemma. Lofty claims are made regarding the results
of inner healing. Popular inner-healing teachers John and Paula
Sandford describe the ministry technique that was initially discovered by Agnes Sanford as being "the key to sanctification"
and the means for developing maturity within the body of
Christ.[10]

In an article published in *Charisma*, Father Dennis Bennett, an
Episcopal priest whose charismatic experience in 1959 is viewed

by many as being the beginning of the modern charismatic renewal, points out that the renewal does not need a "new wave of the Spirit" to bring the body of Christ into maturity. Instead, according to Father Bennett, every Christian, after being baptized in the Holy Spirit, really needs inner healing or soul healing so that the chains of the past can be broken and sanctification and stable maturity can freely develop.[11] Father Bennett's wife, Rita, a popular inner-healing teacher who has written much on the subject, stated in another article in *Charisma* that the charismatic renewal has been held back to some extent because people need to be set free. Such freedom, according to Mrs. Bennett, is produced through soul healing. Her desire is to help heal the church so that it will be strong and whole for the coming of the Lord Jesus Christ.[12]

Inner-healing teachers are zealous to see the purposes of God for the body of Christ brought into fulfillment. Such zeal is commendable. *But zeal must be properly directed and must be based upon truth.* No one questions the past zeal of Jim Jones or of those who sell flowers for Dr. Moon. Zeal not based upon truth leads to great deception, bondage, and heresy. Many of the deceptive teachings exposed by the authors of *The Seduction of Christianity* are examples of misdirected and falsely based zeal on the part of charismatic teachers. In most cases the *motives* of the teachers are not in question, but the *principles and methods* used to produce results are often highly suspect. Is it possible that such is also the case with inner healing?

WHAT DOES THE BIBLE SAY?

Sanctification, spiritual growth, and Christian maturity are very important subjects within the scope of Christianity. The New Testament, particularly the epistles of the apostle Paul, are mainly directed toward spiritual life, growth, and maturity in Christ Jesus. Obviously, any ministry which offers sanctification and which claims to solve the problem of human sin, thereby leading to wholeness for the church of Jesus Christ, must be clearly discerned in the light of Scripture.

The problem of the adverse behavior of Christians is certainly not a new problem. All believers of the past have struggled with the weaknesses of the sinful human flesh. It is not peculiar that such struggle should exist today, even among charismatics. While there are some churches who proclaim the doctrine of perfect sanctification, the experienced reality of this phenomenon is something quite different.

A number of years ago I became friends with a man who was a part of a "perfect sanctification" denomination. From my perspective, if God was giving perfect sanctification to these people, I was willing to go to their church to get it. I asked him, "Do you people really have perfect sanctification?" He responded, "We have the doctrine of perfect sanctification, not the reality!"

The New Testament contains no promise that the struggle against the power of the sinful nature will ever come to an end this side of eternity. While God's Word offers us victory in the midst of the struggle, there are no biblical "quick fixes" leading to sanctification. The apostle Paul clearly depicts the nature of the human dilemma in the classic seventh chapter of Romans. After setting forth the great doctrine of justification by faith and powerfully declaring our union with Christ Jesus in His death and resurrection, the apostle proclaims:

> I do not understand my own actions. For I do not do what I want, but I do the very thing I hate. . . . For I know that nothing good dwells within me, that is, in my flesh. I can will what is right, but I cannot do it. For I do not do the good I want, but the evil I do not want is what I do. Now if I do what I do not want, it is no longer I that do it, but sin which dwells within me (Romans 7:15,18-20).

Inner-healing teachers claim that the ministry they offer to the body of Christ breaks this binding power of sin. Inner healing is seemingly an answer to the "Romans 7 dilemma." Describing what Agnes Sanford discovered in inner healing, John and Paula Sandford state: "She saw and taught that ancient, unforgiven, forgotten sins buried in the heart could be manifested in unwanted, unseemly behavior which could be changed if such sins were forgiven and the heart were cleansed."[13]

There is no basis for this claim in Scripture. The Bible does not tell us that the hurts of the past motivate, cause, or determine our behavior in the present. It would certainly seem that the New Testament, especially the epistles of Paul, which are primarily concerned with the Christian life, sanctification, and growth in Christ Jesus, would provide clear support for the claims of inner healing. This is especially true when we consider that the first-century Gentile Christians entered the church with the baggage of paganism. Yet there is no biblical indication to support the claim that the traumas of the past determine behavior in the present.

By claiming that these hurts of the past are buried within the unconscious mind, inner healing moves from theology into psychology, since the discovery of this alleged unconscious dimension within the human psyche is of recent origin. It is not possible to clearly fit the concept of the unconscious mind into biblical definition, even though inner-healing teachers and others who seek to find a place for the concept of the unconscious in their theology make that attempt.

The New Testament understanding of "the heart" certainly cannot be honestly redefined as "the unconscious," as some suggest. We are to love the Lord our God with our whole heart. The Bible speaks of the "thoughts" of the heart, the "reasonings" of the heart, the hardness of the heart, the purposes of the heart, pondering thoughts in the heart, making melody in the heart, etc. These are *conscious* rather than *unconscious* functions.

Paul Yonggi Cho attempts to equate the apostle Paul's definition of the "inner man" or the "inmost man" (Romans 7:22,23; Ephesians 3:16) with the unconscious mind, claiming that the apostle actually discovered the unconscious 2000 years ago. Cho speaks of the "inner man" as being the "hidden man," equating the concept with "the heart" or "the spirit."[14] Such definitions are a flagrant misuse of the Word of God.

In a later chapter we will spend much more time in dealing with the definition of this very controversial subject of "the unconscious mind." We will see how any attempt at seeking to integrate this questionable concept into Christian teaching results in a smorgasbord of confusion.

We will also discover that the use of visualization or what Agnes Sanford referred to as a "little game in the imagination" is directly related to probing, tapping into, or "crashing" this dimension of the unconscious mind, a dimension which is not found in the Bible but drawn out of psychology.

The initial red flag that the inner-healing teaching raises is the question of the authority of Scripture in the teachings and doctrines of the church. That will be our concern in the next chapter.

The Question of
Biblical Authority

3

The Question of Biblical Authority

The inner-healing teaching is not based upon or drawn from the content of Scripture. The New Testament does not teach that the traumas of childhood, often inflicted by others and buried within the subconscious or unconscious mind, hinder the sanctification, spiritual growth, and maturity of believers in Jesus Christ. The Bible offers no promises and gives no examples of Jesus being available to heal the hurts of the past by "playing a little game in the imagination." Neither the understanding of inner healing nor the methodology of inner healing is drawn from, based upon, or even remotely suggested in the Bible.

The inner-healing teachers reason that there are many things resulting from modern science and technology that are not mentioned in the Bible but are still freely and legitimately used by Christians. They claim that God is the source of all truth, and that whether the truth is theological or psychological makes little difference: "Truth is truth"; "All truth is God's truth." Therefore, to use theories from psychology as the basis for Christian sanctification is acceptable to the inner-healing teachers. Those who reject this notion and accept only teaching based upon Scripture are accused of *fundamentalism or evangelical rationalism.*

THE QUESTION OF BIBLICAL AUTHORITY

The question at stake is vitally important because it involves the crucial subject of *biblical authority*: the place of Scripture in the teaching and doctrine of the church. *Is the Bible the sole source and norm* for all teaching on the ways, means, methods, and purposes of God pertaining to faith and life, forgiveness and salvation, justification and sanctification? Or will God employ extrabiblical teachings and principles drawn from other fields, such as psychology, to offer life, salvation, and deliverance to His people? Will the Holy Spirit develop new methods and techniques for deliverance and healing, or will He simply enlighten our understanding of the basic truths and methods already contained within Scripture?

It is here that lines are drawn and different positions maintained on the basis of denominational theology, specifically the difference between the Protestant and the Roman Catholic position on authority.

This difference may cause potential problems within the charismatic renewal. Leaders within the renewal have sought for years to avoid any distinctions or differences resulting from denominational loyalties, especially between Catholic and Protestant charismatics. Unity has been sought around the commonly shared experience of the Holy Spirit. This has produced the result that truth has become subordinate to unity. Having been a part of the charismatic renewal for over 15 years and having been involved in some leadership roles, I know that *correcting theology* is not widely practiced among charismatic leaders. This creates an invitation to deception, leaving the movement open to many strange teachings.

Differences between Roman Catholic and Protestant theology are very evident in the inner-healing movement. For example, if you read the inner-healing writings of the Linn brothers or Francis MacNutt, Roman Catholic theology is easily discerned. The Linn brothers encourage praying for the dead, and Francis MacNutt speaks of visualizing the Virgin Mary in the inner-healing process. Should not Protestant inner healers be disturbed by these references? In addition, should not the claim that the visualization of the Virgin Mary also "works" to produce inner healing raise questions in the minds of Protestants regarding the very nature of the visualization technique?

In dealing with the subject of the authority of Scripture, there is a clear difference between the Reformation Protestant position and the position of the Roman Catholic Church. While the principle of the Reformation underlined *the sole authority of Scripture in all matters of faith and life*, the Roman Catholic Church accepts the authority of the Papacy and the development of theology through traditions alongside the authority of Scripture.

With this in mind, it is not surprising that the major portion of inner-healing advocates are found within the Roman Catholic Church or within liberal denominations where the authority of Scripture has not been taken very seriously.

TRUTH IS TRUTH?

While it is not surprising that Roman Catholics and liberal Protestants venture outside the biblical boundaries in search of new truth and methods, it is surprising when that practice is espoused by men who are a part of Bible-believing Protestant denominations where the sole authority of Scripture in all matters pertaining to the Christian faith and life is confessed.

Consider, for example, the position suggested by Reformed pastor Robert Wise. Writing in *The Church Divided*, the book released for the purpose of answering some of the claims made by Hunt and McMahon, Wise states:

> It's important to recognize that . . . there is a principle of interpretation at work which violates the correct use of Scripture. Hunt and McMahon pursue the error that unless there is a chapter and verse for any practice, then God forbids the method. There are no chapter and verse for modern surgery, air conditioning, cars or aspirin. The Bible never says clearly that women can participate in the Lord's Supper. Should they be disallowed because the practice does not have a supporting text?[1]

Pastor Wise is stating that the Bible is not a handbook for all knowledge and that we cannot expect to find proof texts supporting and defending all practices before we engage in them. But in his argument Pastor Wise is failing to properly distinguish between different types of *truth, knowledge, and practice*. While there is truth in the principle of the internal combustion engine which propels an automobile, it is not *theological truth*, since it does not define and describe the ways, means, and workings of God to bring life and salvation to His people. Because I am free to use an automobile, which is not mentioned in Scripture, does this mean that I am also free to employ, as a means for sanctification and maturity in Christ, the notion of healing the unconscious mind through a "game in the imagination" in which Jesus is visualized—which is also not mentioned in Scripture?

Richard Dortch, a minister in the Assemblies of God who is presently the executive director of PTL Ministries, echoes the "truth is truth" sentiments in an article published in *Ministries* magazine. He writes:

> At the same time, we cannot cast aside truths just because someone inside the church did not first invent a particular concept. . . . Who is the originator of all truth? Who gave us medicine, healing, knowledge, and energy? Who gave us the greatest Guidebook for all subjects of science, behavior modification and self-improvement? Who sent the Holy Spirit to guide us into all truth? And just because the Bible does not specifically mention computers, psychological techniques, automatic transmissions and telecasts by name does not mean that I must not use them.[2]

I have great difficulty understanding the position of both Pastor Wise and Pastor Dortch over against the unique quality of biblical revelation and the relationship between biblical revelation and theological truth. Is the Bible, according to these men, the sole source and norm of all truth pertaining to the Christian faith and life? Is truth that is discovered within science of the same nature as biblical truth? This is what they are saying! Are these men espousing the position maintained by their church bodies over against the unique quality and sole authority of biblical revelation? In order to fit inner healing and psychological technique into their theology are they not undermining the basic foundation of all theological truth?

In his classic book titled *Protestant Biblical Interpretation*, Bernard Ramm describes the New Testament as "the final, full and clear revelation of God," and "the full revelation of ethical, spiritual, and theological truth." Although, according to Dr. Ramm, the Old Testament is prior in time, "the New Testament is the capstone of revelation." Everything essential to salvation and Christian living is clearly revealed in Scripture. No essential truth, Ramm points out, is tucked away among incidental remarks.[3]

Will God reveal new truth, new methods of reaching Him, new techniques leading to spiritual maturity and sanctification? According to the position maintained within most Protestant and Pentecostal denominations, the answer is a resounding *no*!

When spiritual and theological truth are at issue, Bible-believing Christians have always demanded *chapter and verse*! Such commitment to the authority of Scripture is not fundamentalism or evangelical rationalism but sound theology. Those within Protestantism who use extrabiblical material as a basis for teaching the saving, delivering, healing work of the Holy Spirit are the ones throwing monkey wrenches into the system. To argue that inner healing is not forbidden in Scripture, or to claim that "all truth is God's truth," or to raise up the straw man of biblical silence pertaining to the use of automobiles, televisions, or electric lights is theologically unreasonable.

OPEN-ENDED THEOLOGY

Since the inner-healing ministry is not based upon Scripture, meaningful discussion and dialogue cannot take place. While an advocate of inner healing may claim that the Lord has established the ministry, one who does not accept the ministry may just as legitimately claim that the devil did it. The argument is unable to be settled since there is no objective biblical content against which the inner-healing ministry can be judged.

Discussing inner healing with those who teach the technique is comparable to discussing the bodily assumption of the Virgin Mary with Roman Catholics. Where there is no agreement on authority, there is no basis for discussion. You cannot open the Bible and engage in a healthy debate over the translation and interpretation of key verses, since there are *no key verses*. Inner healing does not possess a doctrinal basis in Scripture. The impasse is simply black and white—one opinion against the other.

Within the denomination of which I am a member, I would not be able to openly teach inner healing or to declare that "all truth is God's truth" without having my theology called into question. This is also true within other Protestant denominations where the singular authority of Scripture is maintained and where theology is taken seriously. The New Testament clearly establishes the position that the correction of doctrine is an important element in the life of the church. Within the epistles, the apostle Paul was continually correcting the false teaching of those who were deceiving the saints.

The inner-healing teachers are for the most part not within a "corrective context." Many are a part of the Roman Catholic Church, where the singular authority of Scripture is not maintained. Some are associated with liberal Protestant denominations, where just about anything goes. Others have left behind their denominational affiliation. All are a part of the charismatic movement, which is far from being a corrective context.

It seems that inner-healing teachers are free to teach whatever they choose to teach. If they choose to redefine the whole body of Christian truth around psychological theories, they are free to do so. In the same way, those who maintain the singular authority of Scripture are free to reject these teachings, write and speak against them, and inform the people of God of the little wolves that have been released into the flock. The debate is an open debate.

Evangelical Protestant churches believe that the Bible is the final, complete revelation of God to man. The Holy Spirit does not come to teach us new truth but to *quicken and enlighten our understanding* of the truth revealed in Scripture. For those who have experienced the ministry of the Holy Spirit, the Bible becomes a new and exciting book. Seeking and discovering truth in the Bible is certainly not an expression of rationalism, since such truth cannot be grasped by mere reason. Only as our hearts and minds are enlightened by the Holy Spirit working through the Word are we able to understand and experience the reality of the Word. Such interplay of the Holy Spirit with the Word of God provides a continually exciting venture into divine revelation.

REMAINING WITHIN THE BOUNDARIES

Personally, I do not accept the legitimacy of any spiritual experience for which I can find no clear basis in the New Testament. My position is not simply the expression of hard-nosed fundamentalistic conservatism, but is based upon a very practical consideration: *I do not want to deceive the people of God who are placed under my spiritual care.* Teaching spiritual experience moves the principle of the authority of Scripture from theology into practice, and the realm of spiritual experience is a vast dimension with many pitfalls. *The boundaries of Scripture provide security from these pitfalls.* The Bible tells us that God has provided for us "all things that pertain to life and godliness" through the knowledge of our Lord Jesus Christ (2 Peter 1:3). If that was true for the first-century Christians, why should it be any less true for us, even in the light of the development of the field of psychology? I know many Roman Catholic charismatics who, for the sake of security, committed themselves to remain within biblical boundaries, even though the theological position of their church is more open-ended. In my opinion, teachers in the church are walking on very thin ice in terms of the judgment of God when they offer spiritual experiences to God's people which are not drawn from Scripture.

When I speak of "basis in the New Testament," I mean *those New Testament promises specifically offering such experience* as well as *New Testament precedent defining the nature and results of the experience.* In other words, I accept as legitimate Holy Spirit experience those truths which can be discovered within the pages of the New Testament by an individual reading it for the first time with no preconceived notions. While such a person, approaching the Word from that position, would discover many legitimate, life-affecting spiritual experiences within Scripture, *inner healing would not be one of them.* Such an approach to Scripture is based upon legitimate principles of biblical interpretation widely accepted within evangelical Protestantism.

WHAT IS THE SOURCE OF INNER HEALING?

Many people within the charismatic movement have examined the inner-healing ministry in the light of Scripture and have rejected it because *it is not in the Bible!* This is a legitimate response and should be expected from those who maintain the position that the Bible is the sole source and norm for all truth pertaining to the Christian faith and life.

Alternatively, many charismatics are open to the possibility that God will develop new forms of prayer and ministry to meet the needs of His people, and they believe that inner healing is or may be an example of that divine development. Some are a part of the Roman Catholic Church or have their roots in more liberal Protestant denominations in which biblical authority is not of prime importance. Many people within the charismatic movement have experienced the reality of the Holy Spirit but have reacted against doctrine and theology, claiming that they are led by the Spirit and not by the doctrinal positions of their church bodies. Many charismatics are new Christians without any roots in denominational theology whatever.

If we are going to do an honest work on the subject of inner healing, we must objectively examine the teaching itself. We cannot say, "It is not in the Bible! End of discussion!" Such a position is not relevant for a wide grouping of charismatic Christians. While I pray that these Christians will remain within biblical boundaries, my purpose in writing this book is not to promote my own position on the question of the authority of Scripture and denigrate the positions maintained by others. My purpose is to evaluate the claims made by those who promote inner healing. In order to do this we must discuss the inner-healing teaching, method, and claims and ask the question, *Are the theories upon which inner healing is based contrary to Scripture?*

Since inner healing is not a biblical teaching, we must seek for the roots of the teaching within the field of psychology. It is here, as we shall see, that inner healing is based. Using principles from the field of psychology as the basis for a Christian ministry raises numerous questions. In addition to the fact that the claims of the inner-healing teachers are not based on Scripture, might the theories from the field of psychology used to construct such teaching be actually contrary to Scripture? Will the Holy Spirit work through these principles to bring healing to the unconscious mind? What are the implications of these teachings drawn from psychology? Can they be integrated into Christian truth without distorting the basic message of the Gospel or undermining the biblical foundation of the faith we share? If the entire church were to accept the psychological concepts and methodology of inner healing, what would be the results?

These questions are of vital importance. It is grossly irresponsible for Christian teachers to visit certain concepts and methods upon the Christian church without recognizing the implications of the teachings or foreseeing the possible pitfalls. While it is true that there are many hurting people in the body of Christ, offering temporal healing accomplishes little if the Gospel, which promises eternal salvation, is lost or diluted in the process.

Freudian
Understanding

4

Freudian Understanding

The basic purpose of psychology is to understand human behavior and answer the question, "Why does man act the way he does?" The goal of psychology is the improvement of the mental and emotional health of mankind by seeking to understand the dynamic of human behavior and to create methodology by which adverse, negative behavior might be adjusted. Episcopal priest Morton Kelsey in his book *Christianity As Psychology* points out that one of the reasons why people become involved in psychotherapy is because they find that they are unable to do the very things they desire to do.[1] Psychology also seeks to provide answers for man's inability to change his own life. This problem, as you recall, was outlined by the apostle Paul in Romans chapter 7.

THEORIES UPON THEORIES

Psychology begins with certain assumptions, the first being that human behavior is generally improvable. The Christian concept of the total depravity of human nature is not acceptable within the field of psychology. Man is not a product of creation and the fall into sin, but is the result of an evolutionary spiral moving him upward toward actualizing his full potential. Textbooks on psychology list the development of Darwin's theory of evolution as being one of the foundation stones upon which psychology is built.[2]

The field of psychology as an independent discipline is a little over a hundred years old, even though discussion regarding the subject of human behavior has always existed within the field of philosophy. The work of Wilhelm Wundt in establishing the first laboratory for the study of human behavior in Leipzig in 1879 marked the beginning of psychology as an accepted study within the social sciences. Only with the establishment of such a laboratory in which human behavior was scientifically evaluated could psychology be legitimately considered scientific. Even at that, it is difficult to discern where theoretical philosophy ends and where scientific psychology begins. It is very important to understand that most of the information offered by psychology is not scientific in nature. Theories proposed within the field of psychology are just that: theories. Martin and Deidre Bobgan point out:

> Learning theories about human behavior and personality is vastly different from knowing facts. . . . Take any text on behavior or personality or psychotherapy and examine it to see how much is subjective theory and how much is objective fact. Then remove all the pages that contain theories and see what remains. In most cases, there would be almost nothing left.[3]

The theories of human behavior proposed by various psychologists involved in research are either rejected or accepted by others within the field. When a number of people accept a specific theory, a *school of thought* develops. There are many schools of thought within psychology, each based upon a specific understanding of human behavior and methodology for the adjustment of behavior. There are few, if any, universally accepted theories within the field of psychology. Each school of thought offers its own unique approach to the human dilemma. There are an estimated 230 different approaches to understanding human behavior.

INNER-HEALING THEORY

The principles behind inner healing are not based upon the Word of God but upon theories from psychology. The question is, Of the 230 different approaches to understanding human behavior found within psychology, which approach forms the basis for inner healing? It would be nice to discover that the concepts upon which inner healing is based were suggested by some born-again, Spirit-filled psychologist who, after spending time seeking the Lord regarding the problem of the binding power of human sin, came up with some notions upon which inner healing was based. While that would not solve the biblical authority problem, it would at least give to the inner-healing ministry some credibility. But this is not the case.

QUESTION: Which school of thought within the field of psychology teaches that *the traumas of the past, inflicted upon an individual during childhood, become buried or repressed within the unconscious mind and eventually cause adverse human behavior?* This is the understanding upon which inner healing is based. Where did the idea originate?

Any person with a primary understanding of psychology is able to answer the question. The principles upon which inner healing is based come from the school of *depth psychology*. The father of this school of thought is the renowned atheist Sigmund Freud!

Agnes Sanford describes the inner-healing ministry conducted by a woman whom she refers to as "Anne." Anne was praying with a friend who was both alcoholic and mentally depressed. In the "visualization prayer" Anne saw herself in a baby's crib and in her mind saw a huge, red, terrifying face leaning over the crib. Her friend to whom she was ministering also saw the face and remembered a time when she was six months old and was startled by her drunken father. Mrs. Sanford went on to explain:

> Anne once related this incident to a group that she was teaching. A psychiatrist, listening in amazement, grew as white as a sheet and gasped, "But that is depth psychology!"
> Of course it is! why not? It is the deep therapy of the Holy Spirit.[4]

For our discussion of inner healing, it is important to understand that the school of depth psychology is merely one school among many. The concepts taught within depth psychology are not generally accepted within the entire field of psychology. There are other concepts proposed within other schools of thought which are contrary to the ideas upon which inner healing is based.

The inner-healing advocates cannot claim that the inner-healing technique is based upon scientific fact and cannot refer to the ideas upon which it is based as "truth." To do so is to claim that the understanding of human behavior proposed within one school of psychology is correct, while the understanding proposed within the other schools of psychology is incorrect. As we will see, Freudian theory is certainly not universally accepted as truth.

DEPTH PSYCHOLOGY

On the basis of his preliminary work with the technique of hypnosis, Sigmund Freud (1856-1939) suggested that human behavior was determined by motivation hidden within the depth of the human psyche, motivation which was below human consciousness. Freud was the first to widely utilize in therapy the notion of the existence of the alleged vast dimension within the human psyche called *the unconscious mind*. Freud used the analogy of the iceberg to describe the unconscious. What is visible above the water is the conscious mind. The far greater mass of the iceberg below the water is comparable to the unconscious mind. Dennis and Rita Bennett use the same analogy of the iceberg in defining the relationship between the conscious and the unconscious. They claim:

> Your subconscious contains all the feelings, thoughts, motivations, that have been recorded through your life. It's been compared to an iceberg. The tip that shows is the conscious part; but like the iceberg, the part under water is seven times larger. There isn't much doubt about the existence of the unconscious mind, but opinions differ as to what part it plays.[5]

For Freud, as also for inner-healing teachers, the unconscious mind contains unresolved, repressed conflicts produced especially during the first five years of life. These repressed conflicts continue to influence if not determine human behavior. The Bennetts explain:

> What is blocked out of our conscious memory will still influence and color our thinking and actions unless it's healed. If an emotional wound is too deep, one cannot merely use intelligence and willpower to solve the problem. Problems in the subconscious are involuntary.[6]

The goal of Freudian *psychoanalysis* is to uncover, through dream interpretation, free association, Freudian slips of the tongue, and various other means, the unresolved conflicts buried within the unconscious mind which allegedly are responsible for producing adverse behavior. The technique of psychoanalysis is highly subjective because it is based upon the analyst's interpretation of the information received.

WAS FREUD RIGHT?

The technique of inner healing is not based upon the validity of biblical authority; instead, it is based upon the validity of "Freudian Authority." Was Freud's understanding of human behavior the correct understanding? Is behavior determined by repressed unconscious content? Do the traumas of the past determine present behavior?

This question can be discussed either from the perspective of psychology or from the perspective of biblical theology. From a theological, biblical standpoint, even if Freud's understanding of human behavior is correct, the question still must be asked as to whether the behavior adjustments which result from the alleged healing of unconscious content are comparable to Christian sanctification. Is the Christian life produced by healing the past or is it a totally new life found in Christ Jesus? Are we to "forget what is behind and press on to the mark of the high calling in Christ Jesus"? Can we "put our hand to the plow and look back"? We will pursue this question in our final chapters, but for now let us consider the claim of the inner-healing teachers that the ministry is based upon "truth." In particular, let us consider the place of Freudian thought within the context of "scientific" psychology.

There are many people within the field of psychology who suggest that Freud was wrong. Martin and Deidre Bobgan point out that there is less confidence in Freudian theory today than ever before.[7] The highly regarded news magazine *Insight* had an interesting article on the growing attack on Freudian theory. The article quoted material from the research of E.M. Thornton, who claimed that Freud's theories were concocted while he was addicted to cocaine and that his central postulate of the unconscious mind did not even exist.[8]

Alternatively, an article in the December 1986 issue of *Psychology Today* indicated that some scientific data coming out of the field of neuroscience seem to confirm some of Freud's cornerstone theories, especially the theory of repression. The article was responding to the claim of Dr. J. Allan Hobson of Harvard Medical School that Freudian psychoanalysis could well be dead by the year 2000.[9] At best, Freud's theories are highly debatable and are far removed from scientific "truth."

Noted Jewish psychiatrist Dr. Viktor Frankl, whose views on human behavior were forged in the death camps at Auschwitz, does not agree with the Freudian view of human behavior. Frankl's approach to human behavior, known as *logotherapy*, depicts man's behavior as motivated by a "search for meaning." Frankl believes that behavior is the result of the conscious choices which we make and is not determined by some unresolved unconscious conflicts. According to Frankl, man is not a victim of his past but is able to detach himself from himself and choose a meaningful lifestyle. Frankl believes that Freud's theories depersonalize man, reducing him to a machine ruled by various unconscious mechanisms.[10]

Frankl also suggested that a deterministic attitude on the part of the counselor will produce the same attitude on the part of the patient. In other words, if inner-healing teachers convince people that their behavior is based upon the unresolved conflicts of the past hidden deep within their unconscious mind, they may be doing more to *produce* neurotics than to heal them.[11]

GOSPEL TRUTH?

Inner-healing teachers have a tendency to accept Freudian theories and present them as if they were gospel truth. Freud contended that dreams reveal the repressed conflicts which exist within the unconscious mind. While this may be true, it is not universally accepted. Actually, there are no scientific data available which prove the Freudian theory of dream causation.[12] While Freud presents a theory, Mrs. Rita Bennett, a popular advocate of the inner-healing technique, states that God often gives dreams to His children to reveal to them what repressed memories within the unconscious mind need healing.[13] Unwittingly, Mrs. Bennett causes God to become an advocate of the school of depth psychology.

Christian leader, inner-healing advocate, and popular author Jamie Buckingham expresses the pleasant desire to dream about Jesus. According to Buckingham, his goal will be accomplished when his unconscious mind is brought under the lordship of Jesus Christ. Sharing his understanding of dream causation, Buckingham states: "Dreams, I knew, are the reflection of our real selves. They are, for the most part, the mirror of our souls—the conscious revelation of the subconscious part of our selves."[14] This raises a very interesting question: How did Mr. Buckingham *know* this reality when science does not know this reality? There are theories of dream causation, but no facts. Yet Mr. Buckingham claims to know. This is simply another example of inner-healing advocates grasping at theories and turning them into facts.

In the newsletter of Father Dennis and Rita Bennett, Mrs. Bennett answers some questions regarding the relationship between inner healing and psychology. She states that she does not indiscriminately accept theories from psychology, but that there are certain truths offered by psychology which she finds very helpful. For example, Mrs. Bennett states that the concept that childhood memories cause us to see God as we saw our earthly fathers has proven true time and again. She points out that many psychological problems are clarified in distinguishing our heavenly Father from our earthly father.[15]

The theory that we see God as we saw our earthly fathers is a Freudian theory. Of course, Mrs. Bennett does not identify it as Freudian. She speaks of it as merely a "psychological concept." As she explains the concept, it would follow that a negative father image would hinder a person from relating to the heavenly Father. Undoubtedly, Mrs. Bennett would use the inner-healing technique to heal the childhood negative memories of the earthly father hidden within the unconscious mind, thus producing a potentially more positive relationship with the heavenly Father.

Dr. Viktor Frankl disagrees with the theory. He points out:

> Moreover, early childhood experiences are not as decisive for the religious life as some psychologists have thought them to be. Least of all is it true that the concept of God is unequivocally determined by the father image. . . . A poor religious life cannot always be traced back to the impact of a negative father image. Nor does even the worst father image necessarily prevent one from establishing a sound relation to God.[16]

The truth may be that there is absolutely no connection between a person's relationship with his earthly father and his relationship with his heavenly Father. If there is a connection, does this mean that a person with a very negative earthly father image has an excuse for his unbelief? Can he be held responsible for rejecting the love and forgiveness of his heavenly Father when his rejection was determined by the type of earthly father he happened to have?

If there were ever a people who brought the baggage of a negative father image into the kingdom of God, it would have been the Christians of the first century. In the Roman, pagan society, fathers owned their families like property and could abuse them in any way they desired. Not only was abortion permitted, but child abandonment was also legal. Yet the New Testament epistles written to these Gentile Christians do not offer even the slightest hint that the traumatic experiences of the pagan past would hinder these new believers from relating fully to their Father in heaven.

What is the basis for the idea that God, our Father in heaven, is an extension of the earthly father image? In *Totem and Taboo* Freud explained his theory of the relationship between God and the earthly father image. Freud did not believe in the existence of a personal God; he was an atheist. He theorized that the concept of God was developed within a primitive cannibalistic tribe who by mistake ate the tribal father. Plagued by guilt, they created a father god to protect them and to be worshiped among them. On the basis of his theories, Freud concluded that ". . . god is in every case modelled after the father and that our personal relation to god is dependent upon our relation to our physical father, fluctuating and changing with him, and that god at bottom is nothing but an exalted father."[17]

SUGAR-COATED FREUD

When reading the inner-healing books, it is important to keep in mind that the authors do not offer blatant Freudian theory. They do not deal with the "repressed perverted sexuality" that has characterized Freudianism, nor do they promote the threefold breakdown of the human psyche into the ego, superego, and id, as Freud suggested. The understanding of human behavior as result-ing from the hurts of the past buried in the unconscious is the major contribution of Freudian theory to the inner-healing ministry.

If you read the inner-healing material, you will find little reference to the person of Sigmund Freud. Inner-healing teachers realize that the name of Sigmund Freud does not elicit a great deal of admiration from the church of Jesus Christ, and rightly so. In addition, Freudian terminology is often difficult to work with. It is not easy to say to someone, "The unresolved conflicts resulting from the parental superego repressing the natural pleasure impulses of the id experienced during childhood are buried within your unconscious mind and produce compulsive, neurotic behavior." Such a statement is not easy to digest.

What you will discover in inner-healing teaching is sugar-coated Freud, offered in such statements as "You have a hurting little child of the past within you." It is far easier for the counselor to define the problem in terms of the "hurting little child of the past" than to speak of "repressed unconscious conflicts arising out of childhood." When you analyze both statements, they mean the same thing.

Most of the inner-healing teachers emphasize the "wounded child within." Rita Bennett's latest book is titled *Making Peace with Your Inner Child*. Throughout their book *The Transformation of the Inner Man*, John and Paula Sandford repeatedly refer to the "inner child." In so doing the Sandfords avoid specific Freudian references to the unconscious mind and psychic determinism. "The wounded inner child" adequately covers all the bases. Ruth Carter Stapleton speaks of the inner child living at the subconscious level.[18]

The concept of the "inner child of the past" is the brainchild of W. Hugh Missildine. Dr. Missildine, a child psychiatrist, discovered in his practice that orthodox Freudian theory and definition were too cumbersome and too far removed from daily experience. Missildine developed new language and concepts in which to wrap the basic Freudian understanding.[19] His approach is a very clever adaptation of Freud that is generally used by the inner-healing teachers.

For our purposes, the "inner child" concept does not change the basic question: Will Freudian theory stand up to the claim that "truth is truth"? Can we import Freud into Christianity and claim that the Holy Spirit will operate in and through Freud's theories to bring healing and sanctification to God's people?

While redefining "repressed unconscious conflicts resulting from childhood" into "the inner hurting child" does not change the question, it does move the adversary position into a new light. It is one thing to come against the theories of the perverted atheist Sigmund Freud, but it is something quite different to come against the "poor little inner hurting child" who needs to be rocked, hugged, and sat upon the counselor's knee.

FREUDIAN SANCTIFICATION

Is it not incredible to suggest that the high ideals of healing and sanctifying the church will be realized by our acceptance of theories proposed by a perverted atheist who, by his own admission, was an enemy of the Christian gospel? Could it be true that Sigmund Freud received revelation that opens our eyes to the manner in which sanctification is able to be accomplished among God's people today, revelation that was hidden from Paul and Peter, James and John?

I find that premise very difficult to accept!

The Bridge to
the Unconscious

5

The Bridge to the Unconscious

"Sanctification, spiritual growth, and spiritual maturity are hindered by the garbage of past experiences deposited within the depth of the unconscious mind." This is the premise upon which inner healing, soul healing, or the healing of memories is based. Such garbage needs to be brought to the surface of consciousness and healed. This is the purpose of the inner-healing ministry.

The premise is clearly derived from the Freudian theories used in psychoanalysis. As we have seen, such theories are not scientific "truth." We are not able to apply the "truth is truth" principle to Freud. Instead we must say, *Theory is not necessarily truth.* The foundation upon which inner healing rests is very unsure.

THE METHOD OF INNER HEALING

Understanding the premise upon which inner healing is based, let us now search out the dynamic of the inner-healing ministry, the methodology for healing the hurts of the past. Such methodology involves visually reconstructing a past traumatic experience and then visualizing the Lord Jesus entering into the situation, bringing His healing love, comfort, and forgiveness.

All of the inner-healing teachers whose material I researched use visualization or imagination in ministering inner healing or soul healing. Agnes Sanford, the founder of the ministry, speaks of "playing a little game in the imagination."[1] Rita Bennett speaks of "visualization prayer."[2] John and Paula Sandford refer to "committed and consecrated imagination."[3] Francis MacNutt counsels "to imagine the harmful incident, and then to imagine Jesus coming into the picture."[4] Ruth Carter Stapleton refers to "faith imagination therapy."[5]

What is the basis for using imagination or visualization in healing the hurts located in the unconscious mind? Where did the idea originate? What does it allegedly accomplish? Does the technique have inherent dangers? Is the technique usable within the parameters of legitimate Christian experience?

THE GIFT OF IMAGINATION

It is important to point out that there is a legitimate, helpful use of imagination in the study and contemplation of the Word of God. The use of the imagination or visualizing adds much flavoring to the Bible, especially in reading the stories surrounding the life and ministry of our Lord Jesus. Having been to Israel on a number of occasions and having seen many of the sites where Jesus walked and taught (especially those sites located around the Sea of Galilee, where the land remains virtually unchanged) has added much to my appreciation of the Gospel accounts. In addition to merely reading and understanding the words, I am able to create a mental image of the situation and surroundings.

Biblical concepts and doctrines are often brought alive through the use of imagination. To see ourselves forgiven of our sins and robed in the perfect righteousness of Christ moves the truth of justification by faith from intellectual concept into a more practical reality. In teaching the truth of Romans 12, in which we are instructed to present ourselves for ministry, I have often encouraged people to imagine such a presentation as they offer themselves to God for service with no strings attached. Such use of imagination effectively applies the Word and promises of God to our lives, but is never divorced from the Word or used as a "technique" which requires the cessation of all thoughts and mental action. Effective teaching and story-telling legitimately combine both the intellect and the imagination.

There is absolutely no reason to suggest that the Word in the imagination is any less effective than the Word in the intellect. Creating the meaning of the Word in our imagination is faith-productive. BUT. . . there is a great difference between what I am describing and the use of visualization in inner healing. If while I am reading the story of Jesus walking on the water I envision the scene in my imagination as I continue to read the biblical account, I am properly using the God-given gift of imagination.

But what if, by emptying my mind of any thoughts or ideas and by concentrating upon that which is being envisioned, I claim that I am seeing the real manifestation of Jesus Himself, who in image form is still able to heal and save as He did while on this earth in the flesh? What if I believe that I can enter into the picture and communicate with Jesus and actually hear His voice and receive His divine wisdom? Am I not at this point moving into a different dimension of visualization? The line between the normal use of imagination and a mystical technique has been crossed!

THE VISUALIZED JESUS

Inner-healing teachers claim that the Person of Jesus visualized in the inner-healing technique is not merely a figment of the imagination but is *objective reality*, coming into the scene from the outside.[6] In other words, inner healing claims that *the visualized Jesus is the real Jesus,* directly healing people as He did during His three-year ministry upon this earth.

Rita Bennett tells the story of a young woman who accepted Jesus through soul-healing prayer. She was confronted by the Person of Jesus in visualization and was thereby saved. Mrs. Bennett claims that a person *does not have to be a believer* in order to get help from Jesus! She contends that Jesus confronts people today in the same way He confronted them while He was upon this earth. The only difference is that Jesus is now manifested through the "visualization prayer." She claims:

> Soul-healing prayer can bring people into the Kingdom who have been turned off by negative teaching, or bad examples on the part of Christians. Jesus Himself

is His own best witness, and when they meet Him and
are healed by Him, like the people in the New Testament, they "follow Him in the way." . . . In soul-
healing prayer, God's omnipresence becomes His
manifest presence.[7]

Remember, when Mrs. Bennett speaks of "meeting Jesus" she
is not referring to an unbeliever coming to faith through the
preaching of the Gospel. She is referring to an individual seeing a
visual picture of Jesus entering into a reconstructed past experience.

While the Bible does tell us that Jesus is the same yesterday,
today, and forever, and that He is with us always, even until the
end of the age, there is no promise or even hint in Scripture that
we are able to find the real Jesus in our imaginations. On the other
hand, the Bible tells us clearly that Jesus comes to us through the
preaching and teaching of the Word, not through some visualization method. In Romans 10:6-9,17 we read:

> The righteousness based on faith says, Do not say in
> your heart, "Who will ascend into heaven?" (that is,
> to bring Christ down) or "Who will descend into the
> abyss?" (that is, to bring Christ up from the dead). But
> what does it say? The word is near you, on your lips and
> in your heart (that is, the word of faith which we
> preach); because, if you confess with your lips that
> Jesus is Lord and believe in your heart that God raised
> Him from the dead, you will be saved. . . . Faith comes
> from what is heard, and what is heard comes by the
> preaching of Christ.

The teaching of the Word of God is very clear as to the means
and method of salvation: We are not saved by seeing some mental
image of Jesus; we are saved by hearing the Gospel. The biblical
prerequisite for salvation and healing is *faith which comes from
the hearing of the Good News of the proclaimed Gospel.* It is for

this reason that the apostle Paul declared, "I am not ashamed of the gospel: it is the power of God for salvation to everyone who has faith."

The claim by Rita Bennett that the real Jesus is discovered in the "visualization prayer" undermines the preaching of the Gospel of Jesus Christ and potentially redefines the entire substance of the Christian faith. If her claim is correct, there is no longer any reason to preach the Gospel. All that is necessary is to lead people into a "visualizing state of mind" to find Jesus. This is not the essence of the Christianity defined in Scripture.

The Bible also clearly informs us that we do not walk by sight but by faith. The apostle Paul writes: "We know that while we are at home in the body we are away from the Lord, for we walk by faith, not by sight" (2 Corinthians 5:6,7).

We also know from Scripture that any appearing or manifestation of the Lord Jesus will not take place until the end of this age. Paul encouraged Titus by saying, ". . . awaiting our blessed hope, the *appearing* of the glory of our great God and Savior Jesus Christ" (2:13). The Greek word used for "appearing" is *epiphaneia*, which is the root of the word "epiphany." The word means "to make manifest." To claim that the omnipresence of God becomes His manifest presence through the "visualization prayer" is to teach contrary to the expectations offered in the New Testament.

In fact, even a legitimate vision of Jesus will not heal or save. Healing and salvation are always based upon faith which claims the benefit offered and promised in the Gospel. We are not healed or saved by an envisioned Jesus entering into our minds in the present. We are healed and saved by the crucified Jesus who shed His blood on the cross nearly 2000 years ago. It is the gospel Word which brings Jesus to us today, not a visualization prayer.

THE MISSING CONCEPT

When you read the claims of the inner-healing teachers about the technique of visualization, you come away with the impression that somehow you have missed some key concept which forms the basis for using visualization to connect the unconscious hurts of the past with the alleged presence of Jesus. This concept, with the potential for revolutionizing the entire Christian faith by leading people into the presence of the real Jesus, has to be based upon something. There has to be some discovery which links imagination or visualization into a dimension where Jesus allegedly exists and is available to help and to heal. If such a notion does not exist, the claim that Jesus can be encountered in the "visualization prayer" sits out in left field, totally unrelated to any other concept. I might just as well claim that marching around the church, shouting "Hallelujah!" and blowing trumpets will also bring Jesus on the scene. In fact, the marching/shouting/trumpet scenario does have biblical support as a method for pulling down walls. The question is, What is the missing ingredient which connects visualization or imagination into the dimension in which we encounter the "real Jesus"?

Since the premise underlying inner healing comes to us from psychology, could it be that the inner-healing methodology—the use of visualization—also comes to us from the field of psychology? Is there a theory in psychology that proposes the use of imagination or visualization as a therapeutic device to reach the hidden hurt in the unconscious mind? If this is the case, referring to visualization as *prayer* is nothing more than a "Christian cover-up," an attempt to wrap psychological technique in verbal piety.

BEGINNING WITH FREUD

In seeking an answer to this question, I discovered, much to my surprise, that the technique of visualization was originally employed in Freudian psychoanalysis. Freud distinguished "primary process thought" from "secondary process thought." The *primary process*, characteristic of early childhood, is composed of visual, memory material. The logical, verbal process, or the "secondary process," according to Freud, developed later in childhood. He believed that "thinking in pictures . . . approximates more closely to unconscious process than does thinking in words."[8]

Mike and Nancy Samuels describe the use of visualization in the early stages of *depth psychology*. They state:

> With the discovery of the function of the unconscious at the turn of the century, man realized that he could get in touch with images within himself of which he had previously been unaware. Both memory and imagination images come from the unconscious. Freud found that a patient who was deeply relaxed or hypnotized could recall images of childhood events they had long forgotten. . . . The images that early psychiatrists were interested in were those memory and imagination ones tied to traumatic emotional experiences.[9]

The technique of visualization came into prominence in the work of Carl Jung. Within the tenets of Jungian analytical psychology we discover many of the answers to the maze of questions raised by the inner-healing technique.

JUNGIAN TECHNIQUE

Carl Jung utilized *active imagination* or visualization as a means for entering into the unconscious mind, but Jung discovered far more within the unconscious than Freud had theorized. Jung uncovered, through visualization or what he termed *active imagination*, a spiritual, mystical element emerging from the depths of the alleged unconscious psyche. He used the term *numinous* to define such content. The term was originally employed by Rudolph Otto, a German theologian and contemporary of Carl Jung. In his book *The Idea of the Holy*, Otto created the term "numinous" to define and describe an experiential confrontation with God and the state of mind accompanying such confrontation.[10] By using the term to describe his visualized experiences, Jung immediately classified them within the metaphysical, spiritual dimension.

Jungian disciples conclude that Jung, by utilizing visualization, tapped into the spiritual dimension. Jungian psychology not only explains the relationship between the use of imagination and the unconscious hurts of the past, but is the obvious basis for the claim that the visualized image of Jesus possesses reality and is not merely a figment of imagination. Jungianism is not only employed within the inner-healing movement to heal the hurts of the past through visualization but is a popular grid for defining and developing one's spiritual life. The writings of Episcopal priests Morton Kelsey (Agnes Sanford's pastor) and John A. Sanford (Agnes Sanford's son) openly promote the theories of Carl Jung as the means for revitalizing one's Christian life and experience. To their credit, neither Kelsey nor Sanford seek to hide Jungianism in verbal piety but clearly attribute their views to the work of Jung. Based upon Jungian theory, visualization advocates claim that they are able to contact "Jesus," be healed by Him, dialogue with Him, and maintain a record in their journals of all the wonderful truths that "Jesus" is revealing to them.

Obviously, it is necessary that we understand Jung if we are to understand the use of visualization within the inner-healing ministry. It is also important to recognize that Jung did not invent the dynamic relationship between visualization and the alleged spiritual dimension; he merely uncovered it and moved it from mysticism and occultism into seemingly legitimate psychology. The relationship between visualization technique and spiritual experience existed long before Jung, especially in Eastern mysticism.

WHO WAS CARL JUNG?

Who was Carl Jung and how did he come to uncover the dynamic relationship between visualization and this "numinous" dimension of the unconscious mind?

Dr. Carl Jung (1875-1961) was a Swiss psychiatrist who began his career as a defender and disciple of Sigmund Freud. By developing the technique of word association, Jung confirmed the

Freudian theories regarding the repressed content within the unconscious mind. Because he supported Freud, Jung became Freud's handpicked successor. Freud wrote to Jung, "You have inspired me with confidence for the future, that I now realize that I am replaceable as everyone else and that I could hope for no one better than yourself, as I have come to know you, to continue and complete my work."[11]

The cordial relationship between Freud and Jung was to be short-lived. In his independent research, Jung discovered that the content of the unconscious was not only comprised of repressed sexual material, as Freud had suggested. Jung theorized that the unconscious also contained religious, mythological material. Freud reacted against Jung's theory and admonished his young disciple not to abandon the sexual theory, but rather to make a dogma of it and raise it up as a "bulwark against the black mud of occultism."[12] These words of the atheist Sigmund Freud were probably the closest he ever came to prophetic revelation.

THE COLLECTIVE UNCONSCIOUS

The central theory of Jungian psychology, that which is often associated with the name of Carl Jung, is the theory of the *collective unconscious*. On the basis of his experience with patients (evaluating the content that often erupted from the unconscious), Jung theorized that there was a deeper level of unconscious content beneath the Freudian personal unconscious. Within this "deep mind" were the memories of the race: its cultural, religious, spiritual, mythological development. Religion for Jung was innate, inbred. He defined the collective unconscious as impersonal and transpersonal, transcending one's own personal experience.

According to the Jungian theory, we are not merely connected to our own personal experiences of the past, but as members of the human race we are also connected to the collective unconscious of mankind and thereby receive a psychic inheritance containing in latent fashion all that has gone on before.

One of Carl Jung's experiences, vital in the establishing of the theory of the collective unconscious, took place in 1906. Jung was walking through the corridor of a mental hospital in Zurich. A young schizophrenic patient, standing by the window in the corridor, beckoned Jung to his side. He told Dr. Jung that he perceived a tube hanging from the sun, swinging back and forth. Out of that tube, the young man claimed, the winds blew. Jung did not think much of the vision, but it did stick in his mind. Four years later, while reading a book describing the rituals of an ancient Greek cult, Jung, much to his amazement, came across the same vision describing a tube hanging from the sun through which the winds blew. How did the young man in the mental hospital receive the same vision as that recorded in ancient occult material? There must have been some unconscious connection between the young man and the mythological concepts of the past. On the basis of this experience and other similar experiences, Jung theorized: The collective unconscious—so far as we can say anything about it at all—appears to consist of mythological motifs or primordial images.[13]

ARCHETYPES

The content of the collective unconscious—the basic themes, motifs, symbols, and perpetually repeated experiences characterizing the human race—Jung referred to as *archetypes*. An archetype is a specific thought form or motif which is a part of the societal psyche, the inherited possession of all peoples. From the Jungian perspective, man did not *learn* the concepts of god, mother, hero, or the wise old man but *inherited* them as acquired psychic characteristics. Jung identified the following archetypes: *anima/animus* (the opposite-sex archetype), *persona* (the mask that people wear), *the shadow* (the evil side of the personality), and *the self* (the true integrated person reflecting perfect wholeness).

The number of archetypes is endless, dependent upon the development of society. For example, if the popular television program "Happy Days" had continued to the point where it became an ingrained part of the human psyche, there would probably develop a *Fonzie archetype*—a hoodlum-type person in a black leather jacket riding a motorcycle. This motif, according to Jungian thought, would be passed on from generation to generation, imparting a specific nuance to the human psyche. While this illustration may appear comical, the concept is accurate.

THE AUTOMATIC FUNCTION OF IMAGES

A basic postulate of Jungian psychology is that the human psyche is healed and developed by way of activating the archetypal content within the collective unconscious through visualization. Developing the archetype produces healing. From Jung's perspective, the psychiatrist did not produce healing but brought the patient into contact with the unconscious content which brought healing. Mike and Nancy Samuels refer to this phenomenon as the *automatic function of images*. They explain the psychological dynamic in this way:

> Releasing an image from the unconscious and bringing it to awareness seems to be a basic growth process in the inner world. The person who experiences such an image is somehow changed by that experience. The person is completed, made whole—it's as if a piece necessary for that person's growth has been found.[14]

Applying this psychological insight to the inner-healing technique eliminates any relationship between inner healing and Christianity. According to Jungian psychology, the *image itself* produces the healing. Therefore the visualization of Jesus, or the Virgin Mary, or Buddha, or Superman would produce the same effect. Each image would have a particular impact upon the personality, dependent upon the archetype being activated and the faith of the individual in the power of the image.

For example, Jung identified the "hero" concept as being one of the main archetypes within the collective unconscious. The hero, the brave man, the warrior, and the avenger are themes that are associated with all peoples, tribes, nations, and generations. It is a part of the collective psyche of the human race. If, for example, a person suffered from a lack of courage and bravery, the development of the "hero archetype" would bring courage and bravery to the personality.

ACTIVATING THE ARCHETYPE

How would a person go about activating the "hero archetype"? Jung believed that the psyche was self-regulating. Eventually, in later stages of life, it would happen automatically, but if a person were suffering from a neurotic lack of self-assertion, waiting for the passing of years to develop the archetype would be neither practical nor highly therapeutic.

As an immediate method of therapy, Jung developed on the basis of his own experience the technique of *active imagination* or what we would call "visualization." If you were the patient suffering from the lack of courage, you would be counseled to sit back, close your eyes, and relax. Seek a passive mental state by eliminating any thoughts, a technique called "centering." Once your mind is relaxed, create in your imagination a "hero figure." You may dialogue with the figure by asking questions, and the imaged figure will respond. You could play fantasy games, depicting this "hero figure" exercising great courage on your behalf. According to Jungian psychology, this exercise would lend courage to your personality.

While the specific motifs within the collective unconscious are the same for all peoples, the manner in which the image of the motif is developed is unique with each individual. For example, Jung claimed that each male possessed the *anima archetype*, the motif of the female counterpart of his personality. Developing that archetype through active imagination would create the individual's ideal woman, the image itself varying from person to person. Entering into a fantasized dialogue with the *anima* would bring greater sensitivity to the personality, leading to a better understanding of women.

The reality of the experience is not found in the image, but in the archetype that is behind the image. In this sense Jung would have agreed with the inner-healing teachers who claim that the manner in which the image of Jesus appears in the imagination makes no difference, since the reality is behind the image and not in the image itself. In other words, dressing up "your Jesus" in tennis shorts does not change the "healing effect" of the technique.

Describing the benefit of the technique of active imagination, Jung's private secretary and dear friend Aniela Jaffe stated: "Often active imagination initiates the cure of neurosis, for it builds bridges between consciousness and previously unacceptable contents of the unconscious."[15] If the content within the unconscious mind is to be reached, it is done through active imagination or visualization.

In *Man and His Symbols*, edited by Jung shortly before his death, M.-L. von Franz, a disciple of Carl Jung, described active imagination as a way of meditating imaginatively, by which a person may deliberately enter into contact with the unconscious and make a conscious connection with psychic phenomena. Von Franz stated that *active imagination* is among the most important of Jung's discoveries.[16]

VISUALIZATION IS ACTIVE IMAGINATION

The use of visualization within the inner-healing ministry is clearly the same as the technique of active imagination developed by Dr. Carl Jung and practiced as a therapeutic technique within Jungian analytical psychology. It is the means for consciously coming into contact with the traumatic experiences and memories which remain buried within the unconscious. It is the bridge from the unconscious into consciousness. Of even greater significance, if this unconscious dimension is equated with the dimension of the spirit, visualization also becomes the bridge to Jesus.

The technique of active imagination or visualization is the same no matter what label is attached to it. Morton Kelsey points out that Carl Jung called the technique active imagination. Others call it psychosynthesis or meditation. The truth is, you may call it anything you wish, but as Kelsey points out, ". . . whatever we call this process, we are still referring to that part of the real world that can be explored by turning inward and using the images dwelling there."[17]

Inner-healing advocates call the process "visualization prayer," "creative imagination," or "faith-imagination therapy." If I wish, I may call it "psychotic fantasy." But the fact is that we are still defining the same thing, though viewing it from a different perspective.

The interesting theory which we learn from Jungian psychology (as it applies to inner healing) is that visualized images are in and of themselves therapeutic. They release content from the unconscious. Carl Jung himself, during a stormy period in his life, discovered that finding the images behind negative, harmful emotions relieved the hurt and brought healing. Merely recalling a traumatic experience from the past and reliving the experience in the imagination is therapeutic. From the Jungian perspective, using visualization in inner healing has absolutely nothing to do with the image of Jesus. It is a purely psychological technique which produces a certain psychological effect regardless of the content of the visualization.

THE OCCULT CONNECTION

In addition to being a technique employed in depth psychology for reaching the unconscious mind, visualization is also used in occultism as a means for "tapping into" the spiritual dimension and contacting "spirit guides" who, according to occultists, provide supernatural insight and wisdom. This "occult connection" is a cloud which hangs over the inner-healing movement, causing the inner-healing teachers to create a defense for the use of visualization against the accusation of occultism.

The fact that Christian teachers who use the technique of visualization must also defend the technique against the charge of occultism should immediately raise questions about the wisdom involved in using visualization. The "occult accusation" cannot be answered from Scripture. There is no clear foundation in the Word of God upon which to base visualization. As we will see, the technique is defended on the basis of questionable logic and false information. The Bible instructs us to "abstain from all appearance of evil" (1 Thessalonians 5:22 KJV). It is certainly true, on the basis of the background of the technique, that the appearance of evil is associated with visualization.

Is Jesus an Inner Spirit Guide?

6

Is Jesus an Inner Spirit Guide?

At this point we could very easily conclude our discussion of inner healing with a clear answer to the question "Is inner healing deliverance or deception?" Consider the following points.

First, *inner healing is not based on Scripture*. The authority-of-Scripture principle is called into question, causing the inner-healing ministry to be unacceptable among a large portion of evangelical Protestants.

Second, by claiming that the real Jesus is available for direct healing and help, the inner-healing advocates *teach contrary to Scripture*. Such teaching undermines the place of the Gospel within the church and is able to potentially redefine the whole body of Christian truth.

Third, the concepts upon which inner healing is based *can hardly be considered scientific truth*. They are questionable theories which are not even universally accepted as truth within the field of psychology.

Fourth, the claims of Jungian psychology indicate that any therapeutic value to be found in the technique of visualization *has nothing whatever to do with Christianity*. The technique is allegedly effective to heal emotional wounds in and of itself.

In any honest debate on the subject of the validity of inner healing within the Christian church, I believe we have enough information to rest our case.

Yet there are still several issues raised by the use of the visualization technique (and by the attempt to integrate the psychological concept of the unconscious mind into the body of Christian truth) that must be discussed. Our discussion from now on must overlap to some degree the area in which Jungian psychology and visualization are being used to introduce a new brand of mysticism or

79

"spiritual discipline" into the church. Many people associated with the inner-healing movement are also proponents of this new mysticism, in which visualization is employed to encounter Jesus and to "fellowship with Him."

THE TECHNIQUE IS THE SAME

Those who promote the technique of visualization in inner healing and in Jungian mysticism claim that through visualization the real person of Jesus Christ is able to be encountered. The problem is: *The same technique of visualization used to allegedly encounter Jesus is used in occultism for the purpose of contacting spirit guides.* Those who teach visualization for Christians have the responsibility to clearly distinguish "Christian visualization" from occult visualization if they expect their teaching to find acceptance within the church. But without the witness of Scripture, providing such clear distinction is impossible. Consider very carefully the line of argumentation used by visualization advocates. You will discover that their reasoning is based either on false information or on faulty logic.

In the newsletter of Father Dennis and Rita Bennett, Mrs. Bennett, answering questions in "An Interview with Rita," claimed that there is a satanic counterfeit of visualization used within occultism, causing well-meaning critics of the inner-healing ministry to equate the counterfeit with the genuine used in inner healing.[1]

But it is not possible to legitimately apply the term "counterfeit" to a technique that does not have a genuine counterpart in Scripture. While we might speak of the counterfeit of speaking in tongues, or define ESP as the counterfeit of the word of knowledge, there is no biblical concept of visualization which can become the object of satanic counterfeit.

Other inner-healing teachers, as well as advocates of visualization as a mystical means for developing one's spiritual life, would not necessarily agree with the "counterfeit" claim of Rita

Bennett. They suggest that there is only a single technique of visualization, but that the variables which distinguish the Christian use of visualization from the occult use are the Christian use of prayer, the spiritual dimension being consciously contacted, the nature of the experience, and the fruit of the experience. We will not discuss in detail the subject of the "fruit of the experience" in this chapter but will deal with that subject in a later chapter.

Inner-healing teacher Robert Wise, in his contribution to the book *The Church Divided*, provides an understanding of the nature of the visualized figure of Jesus used within the inner-healing ministry:

> In the inner world, it is not clear what is good, demonic, or redemptive. The only sure guide into our past is the Holy Spirit. Jesus Christ is Lord of the present and the past, is the perfect one to help us. In contrast to the use of inner guides, prayer involving reconstruction of experiences is not talking to oneself. Jesus Christ is objective reality who comes in from the outside. Rather than making a general foray into the unconscious, He leads us to the specific contents of actual past experience. As we are in touch with our past need, He comes into that situation. . . . Any form of active imagination is a quest to experience the inner world. You are talking to a part of yourself that has been cut off or suppressed. However, if people go into this world seeking the evil one, he can be found.[2]

Robert Wise, a pastor in the Reformed Church, provides an explanation of the visualization technique which confirms the Jungian connection to the inner-healing methodology. He clearly points out that active imagination is used to enter the world of the unconscious, the "inner world."

Wise also informs us that it is not clear whether the content within the unconscious is good, demonic, or redemptive. From his perspective, the variable in the use of visualization is not the nature of the technique but the content of the experience itself.

Because of the uncertain nature of the content which comes forth from this inner world of the unconscious, Wise points out that it is necessary for Jesus to lead to the specific content of past experiences which require His healing touch. While Jesus serves the purpose of being an inner guide, Wise states that the visualized image of Jesus is not of the same nature as an inner spirit guide. From his perspective, the nature of the experience is different. Let us examine this claim.

INNER SPIRIT GUIDES

Ronald Shone, the author of the popular book *Creative Visualization* (published in England), points out that inner spirit guides are visualized figures who come from areas of consciousness outside our conscious experience. Used in occultism, these inner guides allegedly possess knowledge beyond what is known at the conscious level. As Shone puts it, "They are persons from the past, present or future who belong to spheres of consciousness outside the conscious sphere. They can be of either sex and can be young or old. They are extremely knowledgeable, especially about ourselves." Shone also warns that caution is necessary in following the advice given by inner guides. While inner guides will give sound advice, he points out that it is possible to be receiving advice from someone who is not your inner guide.[3]

Jose Silva, the founder of Silva Mind Control, refers to inner spirit guides as "counselors." He states:

> Counselors can be very real to Mind Control graduates. What are they? We are not sure—perhaps some figment of an archetypal imagination, perhaps an embodiment of the inner voice, perhaps something more. What we do know is that, once we meet our counselors and learn to work with them, the association is respectful and priceless.[4]

The person meditating welcomes the inner guide or counselor into the visualization process. A "centered" mental state in which thoughts are set aside in order to receive images is a necessity for calling upon the inner guide. The inner guide may be a person from history. Jesus, Mary, Buddha, or any other spiritual leader may be chosen. Once the inner guide is "seen" in the imagination, dialogue begins. Questions are asked and the inner guide gives answers. Those who advocate the use of inner guides claim that the guides often reveal wisdom and insight of which the recipient had no previous conscious knowledge. Often the use of inner guides includes journaling or keeping a "private diary" of the wisdom received from the inner guide.

The popularity of the visualization technique, including psychic interface and dialogue with inner guides, creates a very interesting situation in the church. Christians who might become involved in mind control or consciousness-expanding teaching (and through visualization contact inner guides) may readily choose the person of Jesus to be their spirit guide. The simple statements "Jesus is my Lord" or "I am being led by the Lord" become open to a completely new interpretation. By that statement one may actually mean "Jesus is my inner guide, my wonderful counselor, and I submit to the direction that I receive in our dialogue."

It is important to note that the visualized Jesus spirit guide is not the real Jesus of history. He is "another Jesus" who may be a mere figment of imagination, or possibly a demonic counterfeit. The question is: Is the visualized figure of Jesus used in inner healing any different in nature and origin from the "Jesus" chosen as an inner spirit guide in occultism?

Carl Jung would disagree with the assessment of Robert Wise concerning the nature of inner spirit guides. Wise claims that the difference between the visualized Jesus and the visualized inner spirit guide is that the figure of Jesus possesses objective reality, whereas the inner spirit guide is merely a psychological reflex or simply people talking to themselves. Carl Jung described his inner guide as possessing objective reality and giving to him unique and superior insights. Jung described the experience as numinous or transpersonal, meaning that the experience possessed spiritual, transcendent quality. In other words, it was not of this world.

In his classic work *The Varieties of Religious Experience*, psychiatrist and pragmatist philosopher William James provides an interesting explanation for the claims of both Pastor Wise and Carl Jung that visualized figures possess objective reality and seem to enter the visualized scene "from the outside." James, writing at the turn of the century before the theories of Freud or Jung became prominent, states regarding religious experience emanating from the unconscious:

> The theologian's contention that the religious man is moved by an external power is vindicated, for it is one of the peculiarities of invasions from the subconscious region to take on objective appearances, and to suggest to the Subject an external control. In the religious life the control is felt as "higher"; but since on our hypothesis it is primarily the higher faculty of the hidden mind which are controlling. . . .[5]

According to James, the objective reality is a mere appearance, characteristic of the content emanating from the subconscious mind.

THE WISDOM OF PHILEMON

One of Carl Jung's popular fantasy figures was the image of Philemon, his development of the wise-old-man archetype. Jung claimed that Philemon possessed objective reality and brought to him, through his visualized dialogues, knowledge of which he had no previous consciousness. Jung referred to Philemon as his "ghostly guru." Philemon became Jung's inner spirit guide. He began journaling in his famous "Red Book" his dialogues with his inner figures in order to keep a record of his psychic processes. Describing the nature of the figure of Philemon, Jung stated:

> Philemon and other figures of my fantasies brought home to me the crucial insight that there are things in the psyche which I do not produce, but which produce themselves and have their own life. Philemon represented a force which was not myself. In my fantasies I held conversations with him, and he said things which I had not consciously thought. For I observed clearly that it was he who spoke, not I.[6]

On the basis of the research conducted by Carl Jung, the visualized image of Jesus used in the inner healing is of the same nature as the visualized inner spirit guides used in mind control or in other occult practices. The required "centered prelude" is the same. The active-imagination technique is the same. The objective reality of the image is the same. The reception of superior wisdom and insight is the same. The numinous inspired nature of the experience is the same.

BUT WE ARE SEEKING JESUS

Inner-healing teachers claim that the major difference is that they are not seeking some inner guide, but are seeking Jesus. They are praying in the name of Jesus. Wise states:

> When we pray in the name of Jesus, we are asking for God to be with us and to make us whole. No one who reaches out to the Spirit of God and seeks contact with His holy person will ever be misled. . . . As we ask Him by the power of the Holy Spirit to speak healing words to us, we can be assured that the voice of Jesus has integrity.[7]

The explanation by Wise is a typical argument put forth by visualization advocates in defense of the technique. Peter Davids in his defense of visualization suggests that it is a neutral technique. It can be pointed at God's door or it can be pointed at the devil's door. The variable in the use of the technique is *whom are you seeking*?[8]

These advocates of visualization apparently assume that occultists *purposely seek the devil.* Such is certainly not true. With the possible exception of a small group of deeply deluded Satan worshipers, nobody in his right mind would purposely point visualization at the devil's door. Occultists—those involved in the pursuit of psychic phenomena and paranormal experiences— honestly believe that they too are finding God and are touching the reality of Jesus.

If you read occult visualization material, such as the little volume *Creative Visualization* by Shakti Gewain or *Centering* by Laurie and Tucker, it is evident that Christians are encouraged to use the name of Jesus and to employ all elements of their Christian faith (including prayer for the power of the Holy Spirit) in their pursuit of spiritual reality through visualization.

For the purpose of trying to find the answer to the question "Do occultists seek the devil?" I browsed through a book describing the religious life and experience of Edgar Cayce. He is probably regarded as having been the most renowned occult psychic. His writings comprise a good portion of the material contained in the "occult" section in local secular bookstores.

In reading about his religious life, I was amazed. This man taught the adult Bible class in an orthodox Protestant church for nearly 24 years. He sincerely believed that in his mystical, psychic trances he was coming into contact with Jesus. Edward Cayce was seeking Jesus! The "source" who spoke through Cayce offered many "prophetic" insights into the deep mysteries of the Christian faith. Cayce accepted the doctrine of the trinity and confessed the historic creeds of the church.[9]

It is not a valid, factual argument to claim that Christians point their visualizing at Jesus while occultists point the technique at the devil. Such is definitely not the case.

If a Christian became involved in some element of occultism and desired to have Jesus as a visualized spirit guide and prayed in the name of Jesus that his image would appear in the imagination, the experience would be *no different* from that of the visualized figure of Jesus employed in inner healing. The major arguments set forth by the inner-healing teachers to defend the use of the technique within the Christian context and to distinguish it from occultism are neither reasonable nor factual. From what I can determine on the basis of research, *there is no difference.*

A Very Dangerous Journey

7

A Very Dangerous Journey

At times the proponents of visualization warn about the dangers that are involved in using the technique. They claim that both good and evil content and that both God and the devil can be encountered in this inner world of the unconscious entered through visualization. Robert Wise states that sometimes it is difficult to determine whether the content from the inner world is redemptive or demonic.[1]

Regarding the dangers of encountering the unconscious inner world Morton Kelsey states:

> The dangers of playing around with the unconscious, with spiritual reality, may be harder to grasp than the tangible dangers of playing with an automobile, or with war or atomic energy, but they are just as real. Whether one uses the Ouija board for thoughtless fun . . . or tarot cards just to relieve the boredom of a rainy afternoon, these ways of reaching unconscious or psychoid experience are capable of opening a person to levels of spiritual reality that are more than can be handled.[2]

Within the category of techniques which tap into this unconscious inner world Kelsey of course includes visualization. He points out that by entering the unconscious one will encounter deep darkness and evil. He equates the opening of the inner world of the unconscious with opening "Pandora's Box." Once it is opened, it is very difficult to close it again.[3]

Assembly of God pastor Mark Virkler became involved in visualization by attending an inner-healing seminar. Probably influenced also by the writings of Morton Kelsey, Virkler promotes Jungian visualization and journaling in his book *Dialogue With God*. While Virkler masks the roots of his teaching by wrapping them in Christian terminology (never mentioning the psychological unconscious), he does state that in dialoguing with God it is possible to get the voice of God "mixed up with the voice of Satan."[4]

CARL JUNG'S QUESTIONABLE SANITY

Carl Jung realized firsthand the dangers involved in the use of active imagination. There was a period in his life from 1913 until 1917 (following his traumatic break with Freud) in which Jung thought of himself as engaged in a voluntary exploration of his own inner world of the unconscious. During this time he experienced numerous encounters with the dead. In 1916 he wrote the ghastly "Seven Sermons to the Dead," the first line of which was received from a "screeching chorus of ghosts" who visited his home one Sunday afternoon. On one occasion, after being involved in a vision in which he and a "brown-skinned savage" murdered a mythological Germanic hero, Jung was so overcome with disgust that he contemplated suicide. He heard a voice telling him that he must immediately interpret the vision or else kill himself with the loaded revolver he kept in his night-table drawer.[5]

Christopher F. Monte, the author of a college textbook on the theories of personality, points out that Jung's experiences during the stormy seven-year period are evidences of "psychotic disorganization." Monte states that there are two schools of thought regarding Jung's venture into the inner world. On the one hand, Jungian disciples claim that Jung's experience represented a "careful and deliberate voyage of exploration." From their perspective, Jung was a visionary who courageously and skillfully "charted unknown psychological realms." Alternatively, there exists an equally certain conviction that Jung's voyage was "not visionary but psychotic, not voluntary but uncontrollable."[6]

NO COUNTERFEIT FOR EVIL

In spite of the dangers involved, the technique of visualization is being widely promoted within the Christian church, especially within the charismatic movement. In addition to the inner-healing teaching, workshops on "centering prayer" or "conversing with God" openly teach Christians how to visualize and reach "Jesus." In many of these weekend seminar experiences, clear warning about the dangers involved in using the technique of visualization is not given. Books on inner healing, offering visualization as a means for reaching and healing hurts buried within the unconscious, usually do not warn that the use of the technique has accompanying dangers.

In considering these dangers and the possibility of deception, it is important to understand that the Bible tells us that the devil is able to parade as an angel of light. It does not tell us that the Holy Spirit will parade as a demon of darkness. When demonic evil is encountered, there is no possible counterfeit: *You are dealing with the real thing.* But if you encounter a numinous spiritual experience, filled with glory and light, *the possibility of a counterfeit always exists*, especially if the method by which that experience was encountered is not based upon any objective biblical truth.

GOD AND THE DEVIL IN THE SAME DIMENSION?

The dangers involved in visualization are based upon the concept that good and evil, the Holy Spirit and demons, and God and the devil exist within the same inner spiritual world of the unconscious entered through visualization. This is a basic postulate of Jungian psychology. Jung taught that confronting the evil within, defined as the "shadow archetype," is a necessary step in the growth process. Only by first passing through "the shadow" could one experience the positive content of the inner world. The first few pages of the book *Resurrection* by Morton Kelsey include a dialogue between Kelsey and the devil as a prelude to a resurrection experience.[7]

Jung applied this same mixture to God. His view of the psychic growth process as being a confrontation between opposites from the inner and outer worlds led him to the conclusion that in God there must also be opposites. In his essay *Answers to Job*, Jung suggested that evil existed within God. Theologically, he preferred to speak of a *quaternity* which included the devil rather than a *trinity* of God.

Wallace Clift in his book *Jung and Christianity* points out that this element of Jungian thought presents the greatest challenge in the attempt to reconcile Jungianism with Christianity.[8] His apprehension is well-founded, especially in the light of 1 John 1:5,6: "This is the message we have heard from him and proclaim to you, that God is light and in him is no darkness at all. If we say we have fellowship with him while we walk in darkness, we lie and do not live according to the truth."

The suggestion that good and evil, God and the devil exist within the same dimension to which we have access through visualization is contrary to biblical teaching. Light and darkness cannot be mixed within the same container. The kingdoms are distinct. We have been delivered from one and translated into the other. I cannot imagine God saying to us, "Children, here is a new prayer technique that I am bringing to you. But be careful! In seeking me through this new method of prayer, you may find the devil."

But merely for the sake of argument, let us entertain this notion that both God and the devil dwell within the same dimension of the unconscious entered through the visualization technique. Should this not also work in our favor? If it is possible to enter this inner world looking for God and finding the devil, might it also be possible to look for the devil but inadvertently stumble upon God? If there is a danger that Christians might turn into occultists by entering the inner world, might occultists, by using the technique of visualization, turn into Christians? If Jesus is able to be discovered within this inner world, is there any evidence that

Buddhists and Eastern mystics found Jesus and came to a living faith in Him through the technique of visualization?

When you consider the fact that there are over 200 million visualizing Buddhists who regularly enter the inner world, there must be some evidence to indicate that at least one or two open-minded seekers found Jesus in this way and became Christians. Are the adherents of Buddhism warned by their spiritual leaders that the danger exists that in their meditations and visualization they may encounter the Christian Jesus and be converted? Obviously not!

IS THIS MERE DELUSION?

From a purely scientific perspective, the question must be raised as to whether meditative visualization actually contacts any entity outside of the one doing the meditating. Are we simply dealing with the reflex of one's own psyche, or, as Robert Wise put it, are people merely talking to themselves? The closest we come to scientific investigation is in the work of Carl Jung. Jung, seeking to remain scientific throughout, sought to explain everything in terms of the theory of the collective unconscious.

If we occupy the position that modern-day Christian mystics are merely pictorially examining their own psyche and that the "Jesus" in inner healing is a simple figment of the imagination, why is the experience seemingly numinous, metaphysical, and otherworldly? Why do occultists claim, as we will see in a later chapter, that moving down to the meditative state opens up the dimension of psychic, supernatural experiences such as ESP, psychokinesis, clairvoyance, and the like? What is there within man that produces such experiences, *or is it within man*? Are we dealing with demonic deception? Carl Jung discovered the same supernatural phenomena emanating from "the unconscious" and wrote much on the theme of *synchronicity*—psychic connections between separated people. He again explained this psychic reality on the basis of making contact within the collective unconscious.

The explanation provided for such phenomena by both occultists and "Christian" visualizers is based upon the existence of the dimension called the *unconscious*. Does such a dimension really exist? Is it a scientific fact? Where did the idea originate?

The Cult of
the Unconscious

8

The Cult of the Unconscious

I mentioned previously that researching the inner-healing ministry opens up a maze of deception. In these next three chapters we will look at that maze of teachings and theories borrowed from psychology and visited upon the church of Jesus Christ. But I assure you that there is light at the end of the tunnel: The last few chapters will present refreshing truth from God's Word about the new life we can live in Christ Jesus.

The ministry of inner healing is directed at the alleged problems existing within the *unconscious or subconscious mind*. Inner-healing teachers claim that Jesus "enters into the unconscious mind" to clean up the residue of the past and produce sanctification. Visualization is the bridge into this dimension.

SCIENTIFIC CHRISTIANITY?

This concept of the unconscious, particularly as it relates to theology, is highly controversial and very confusing. Through the concepts of Jungian psychology, religious experience is able to be defined as emanating from the unconscious or the collective unconscious. The claim for the scientific validity of depth psychology seems to place a scientific foundation under religious experience and under many elements of Christian theology. At least, it appears that this is the motive behind the attempt to integrate the concept of the unconscious into Christian teaching. As we will see in the next chapter, Agnes Sanford attempted to explain elements of redemption in terms of "Jesus entering into the collective unconscious of the human race."

Seeking to lend scientific credibility to religious experience by explaining it in terms of the unconscious mind or subconscious self is not a new practice. In fact, psychiatrist and pragmatic philosopher William James, in his book *The Varieties of Religious Experience* (written at the turn of the century, before the theories of Freud and Jung became popular), suggested that the "subconscious Self" may be the very concept needed to scientifically understand the dimension of religious experience. According to James, understanding religious experience as emanating from the depths of the inner self will "preserve a contact with 'science' which the ordinary theologian lacks."[1]

The search for the validity of the faith we proclaim is seemingly culminated in the profound discovery of the unconscious mind . . . *or is it*? Might it also be true that using the concept of the unconscious to undergird the Christian faith and experience will distort and ultimately destroy the basic proclamation of the Gospel and the biblical understanding of our faith? Some innerhealing teachers claim that "the real Jesus," being allegedly discovered within the unconscious, is available to help and to heal apart from the Gospel proclamation. Those who promote visualization as a mystical form of meditation claim that, within this dimension of the unconscious, Jesus can be encountered, His voice heard, His wisdom directly received. Teachers in the church who use visualization to create "miracles" believe that the unconscious is a storehouse of supernatural creative power.

Obviously, because of the vital implications involved in integrating the concept of the unconscious into Christian truth, clear thinking in this area is very important. Red flags need to be raised where necessary. Christian teachers who advocate visualization as a means for reaching Jesus do not want to build their theology upon a mere figment of imagination or a demonic counterfeit. I believe that such is already happening within the inner healing/visualization movement.

"I AM NOT CONSCIOUS OF IT"

In dealing with this subject of the unconscious it is very important to think clearly in order to distinguish a simple *definition* from a mystical *dimension* and *factual reality* from *assumption and theory*. The followers of Freud and Jung have had a tendency to exaggerate the theories of the "masters," finding far more in their concepts than what Freud or Jung originally intended.

If someone would ask you the question "Is there such a thing as the unconscious mind?" you might legitimately answer "I don't know. I am not conscious of it." Seeking a definition for something of which we are not conscious will produce problems. How is something to be defined if there is no conscious awareness of the thing itself? From a purely philosophical standpoint, knowledge of the unconscious is nonattainable. Once you become conscious of it, it is no longer *unconscious*. The very nature of the thing defies definition. The actual existence of "the thing" is always (and must be) theoretical.

THE NONOBSERVABLE HUMAN PSYCHE

It is not possible to examine the human psyche and thereby discover the unconscious mind. All that is able to be examined are the mental processes that emanate from the human psyche, leading to the theory that something unconscious exists. The psyche, the thing itself, is not perceivable. All concepts employed within the framework of the study of the psyche are *definitions and descriptions* of the psychical processes.

For example, Freud discovered (especially through the use of hypnosis) that there were elements contained within the human psyche of which the subject was not conscious. Jung claimed to discover that there are elements shared by the human race and contained within the human psyche of which the individual person was *not conscious* and of which the human race as a whole was *collectively not conscious*. So to begin with we are simply dealing with definitions or descriptions of alleged mental processes.

Freud and Jung built their systems upon the theory that these nonconscious elements within the human psyche possessed a dynamic, in that they influenced (if not actually determined) human behavior. This is called "psychic determinism." From the Freudian perspective, unconscious content was created by "repression." The line between the conscious and the unconscious was always fluid and changing. Once repression was removed, the content moved from the unconscious into the conscious.

All that can be said about the terms *unconscious* and *collective unconscious* is that they are definitions of alleged mental processes which are supposed to dynamically influence human behavior. No more can be said, unless someone discovers a method whereby the human psyche is able to be extricated from the personality, placed under a microscope, observed, and divided into various neat compartments. Of course such an analysis is not possible.

Within the development of Freudian thought, problems arose regarding the use of the concept of *the unconscious*, leading to an adjustment in definition and terminology. Initially, the concept of *unconscious* was simply descriptive in nature. In seeking to structure and delineate the various systems or elements within the human psyche, Freud originally used the concept of the unconscious, but soon discovered that it created confusion. He replaced it with the concept of the "id" to denote repressed drives in conflict with the "superego." The concept of "unconscious" again became merely descriptive.[2] It was used by Freud as an adjective, not a noun.

FROM DEFINITION TO DIMENSION

Inner-healing teachers give the impression that these definitions of mental process are in fact *dimensions* or *compartments* within the human personality. If a person were able to invade the human psyche and journey through its vast regions, inner-healing teachers seem to think that a door marked "THE UNCONSCIOUS" would be discovered. Upon that door Jesus is knocking. If the journey proceeded further, into the "deep mind," another door marked "THE COLLECTIVE UNCONSCIOUS" would become visible. As we will see, Agnes Sanford taught that Jesus entered into that *dimension*. Creating such compartments within the human psyche is more science fiction than scientific fact. What began as *the definition of a dynamic* becomes *the creation of a dimension*.

If you read the writings of Morton Kelsey, you will discover some neatly composed line drawings defining the various dimensions within the human personality based upon the understanding of Carl Jung. Somehow, after reading a great deal of Jungian philosophy, I get the impression that Jung would not necessarily agree with such clear delineation. As a scientist, Jung understood that the psyche was nonobservable. The limits of legitimate scientific research stopped at the definition of observable mental process. He pointed out that nothing could really be said about the collective unconscious.[3]

Using Kelsey's material, inner-healing teacher Father Ted Dobson states that for Jungian advocates the "existence of *THE* collective unconscious is beyond doubt."[4] While Jung believed that mankind was *collectively unconscious* of specific elements, Morton Kelsey, Ted Dobson, Agnes Sanford, and inner-healing advocates in general turn the definition into "a thing," a dimension, a place within the human psyche. This same transformation of Freudian/Jungian definition into some mystical dimension takes place among occultists, New Age advocates, consciousness expanders, and the like.

"THE THING"

Once we have "a thing," a "cult of the unconscious" readily comes into being. The games begin! Every mystical element associated with human existence is able to be explained in terms of "the unconscious." Christians jump on the bandwagon. They are now able to explain in "scientific" terms what the world calls "supernatural silliness," such as being born again or experiencing the power of the Holy Spirit. Agnes Sanford, for example, defined speaking in tongues as the known languages of mankind coming forth from the collective unconscious as the result of a spiritual experience.[5] Christian leader Paul Yonggi Cho claims that the unconscious is fourth-dimensional and has supernatural powers within it. By pushing visions into this container man is enabled to work miracles. In the foreword to one of Cho's books, Dr. Robert Schuller says, "Don't try to understand it. Just start to enjoy it! It's true. It works! I tried it!"[6] Norman Vincent Peale is enabled to add *Positive Imaging* to positive confessing, claiming that once our visions get into the unconscious all kinds of supernatural power is released.[7] Inner healers suggest that "the thing" needs healing, for Jesus wants to get into *the unconscious* and clean things up.

DIFFICULT DEFINITION

One of the major areas of confusion that exists within the inner-healing movement involves the definition, in terms of biblical concepts, of this unconscious mind which is the object of the healing in "inner healing." How is this "thing" to be fit into Christianity without losing the flavoring of legitimate Christian orthodoxy? In this area, inner-healing teachers admittedly disagree. It is of course very understandable that the attempt to define such a nebulous entity as "the unconscious mind" would cause numerous problems and disagreements. The task is not easy: Inner-healing teachers are struggling to define something that is already a definition of that which is nondefinable.

Dennis and Rita Bennett have little doubt about the existence of "this thing" but refrain from equating the unconscious with the dimension of the spirit. They think of the unconscious as being a part of the soul. From their perspective Jesus does not dwell in the unconscious but dwells in the "spirit." Through "soul healing" Jesus moves from the spirit into the soul to bring His healing work. They state:

> There isn't much doubt about the existence of the unconscious mind, but opinions differ as to what part it

plays. Some think God comes into the soul by way of
the unconscious. Some would say the unconscious *is*
the spirit. We don't believe this is the right way to look
at it. God does not enter the personality through the
depths of the unconscious, but from a totally different
direction. The spirit is not the unconscious mind. The
unconscious is part of the soul.[8]

While the Bennetts' definition is an attempt to keep their
theology orthodox, their method of using active imagination to
adjust alleged unconscious content remains the same. Remember, the Bennetts claim that Jesus is "knocking on the door" of the
unconscious mind.

But if you compare the Bennetts' understanding of the definition of the unconscious with the views of Father Ted Dobson, you
note a drastic difference. Father Ted believes that visualization is
the window *into the spirit* and equates the unconscious with the
spiritual dimension, claiming that the unconscious mind exists
within an eternal dimension. He believes that our real lives are
hidden with Christ within that spirit dimension. Dobson's understanding is essentially the same as (and is in fact based upon) the
concepts of Morton Kelsey as set forth in his handbook on
meditation and visualization, *The Other Side of Silence.* While
the Bennetts say that God does not enter through or dwell within
the unconscious, Dobson claims that the unconscious is an eternal
dimension in which Jesus dwells. He states.

For it is only our consciousness and our bodies that
live in the realm of space and time; our unconscious
which is our spirit lives out of the realm of time, in
eternity, as does Jesus and his Father and the Spirit.
This fact may be difficult for us to imagine, but our
difficulty makes it none the less true.[9]

Since the inner-healing teachers generally attribute the founding of the inner-healing ministry to Mrs. Agnes Sanford, you would think that the books by Agnes Sanford would provide a clear definition of the relationship between God, the unconscious, and visualization. Not so. Reading the works of Agnes Sanford with an eye out for clear definition can be a very frustrating experience. Her simple, folksy style does not lend itself well to defining concepts. Mrs. Sanford seemed to possess minimal sensitivity to the theological implications of some of her theories.

If you read her material asking the question "What is the unconscious?" this is what you encounter:

> But this much I do know: that this unseen part of me, whether submerged beneath the depths of my conscious self or rising above it, whether descending into hell or ascending into heaven, this also is myself. And if I am to be a whole person, this area of emanation or interpenetration must also be healed. I call this part of me the soul, or the "psyche." I might instead say "the unconscious" or "the subconscious," or "the deep mind" or the "spirit."[10]

While Dennis and Rita Bennett clearly distinguish the soul dimension from the spirit dimension and point out that it is a very important distinction, Mrs. Sanford lumps it all together. Actually, Agnes Sanford seemed to possess far more wisdom than some of her disciples who try to precisely nail down a concept that is unknowable. While her definition does not lend itself to the establishing of a clear theological context, she certainly does succeed in covering all the bases.

Within inner healing there is a wide diversity of definition which is very confusing. Some proponents say that the unconscious is to be associated with the soul and speak of "soul healing" rather than "inner healing." Others, such as John and Paula Sandford, refer to the unconscious as being "the heart" or "the inner man." Some equate the unconscious with the spiritual dimension through which God enters and dwells within the life of the Christian. Still others, according to a recent article in *Charisma*, suggest that "this thing" which is called the unconscious or the collective unconscious is in fact *God Himself*![11]

Attempting to define this concept of the unconscious mind and to relate it to some existing biblical dimension such as the "spirit" or "soul" or "inner man" or "heart" (or for that matter God Himself) is virtually impossible. It is a senseless task. The concepts simply do not connect.

A FAIRY TALE

In the human makeup it is certainly true that there are vast elements within the mind which are not a part of moment-by-moment consciousness. The brain has the capability to store virtually innumerable bits of information. Only a small portion of that information is a part of present consciousness. Of most of it we are certainly *unconscious*.

But to create a mystical container for these unconscious elements which physiologically are simply stored in the memory banks of the brain and to turn the descriptive adjective "unconscious" into a dimensional noun "the unconscious" is to take a rather large leap. The existence of unconscious content within the psyche does not imply the existence of *the unconscious*. To claim that through the technique of visualization one enters the dimension of the unconscious or to suggest that Jesus is knocking on its door or has already entered it and can be found inside is to create a fairy tale. Rod Serling's creation of "The Twilight Zone" to explain seemingly illogical events has as much credibility as the mystical dimension of "the unconscious."

IF NOT THE UNCONSCIOUS . . .

If there is no such dimension as the unconscious mind, and if the concept is not able to be used as a mystical catchall, the question must still be asked, What is within man that produces seemingly supernatural, mystical experiences through meditative visualization? The classic work of William James *The Varieties of Religious Experience* confirms what Carl Jung also discovered: Man, turning in on himself via meditative technique, does experience what appears to be objective, supernatural content. But to say that the inward turn enters the unconscious, the subconscious, or the collective unconscious is mere guesswork. But if introverted mystics are not entering the unconscious, what are they getting into?

Might it be that man, searching for God within himself, taps upon the door of the demonic dimension? This whole theory of the unconscious may have been contrived in the pits of hell. If one does not feel comfortable with this possibility, might it instead be that meditative, visualizing man is merely dredging the depths of the perverted human nature, bringing up the "works of the flesh," which include heresy and witchcraft?

There is at least as much evidence to support these views as there is to support the claim that the experience is based in the unconscious or the collective unconscious. When we consider the fact that Freud's first confrontation with the alleged unconscious dimension came through the use of hypnotism and that Jung's first clue to the collective unconscious came by comparing the hallucinations of a schizophrenic with the visions manifest in ancient occultism, we are left with the distinct impression that some outside influence is involved. Reading the account of Carl Jung's seven-year sabbatical of mysticism leads one to believe that he was entertaining demons rather than charting a brave new course through the inner recesses of the unconscious. In fact, during this time he received a personal visit from a screeching chorus of ghosts.

Using the fairy-tale concept of "the unconscious" to explain Christian experience or to promote an understanding of the sanctification process certainly opens a can of worms. But we are only beginning to unravel some of the maze associated with a religion derived from "the unconscious." Would you believe that using the drug LSD will bring us into the presence of God within the unconscious? In using this drug do we have, as Timothy Leary suggested some years ago, a new sacrament emerging?

God and the Unconscious

9

God and the Unconscious

Is God able to be found within this mystical, fairy-tale dimension of the unconscious mind? Is the unconscious mind to be equated with the eternal, spiritual dimension in which God dwells? Does God—Father, Son, and Holy Spirit—actually reside within the deep mind of every person, able to be reached by visualization or by other means of altering consciousness? Inner-healing teacher Father Ted Dobson claims that this is so:

> . . . our unconscious, which is our spirit, lives out of the realm of time, in eternity, as does Jesus and his Father and the Spirit.[1]

The late Agnes Sanford certainly thought that God was able to be reached within the unconscious mind. She wrote:

> Yet there is hope, because God Himself is intricately involved with time and Time, and because seeing our need, He incarnated Himself and became man, thus entering into the collective unconscious of the race: into the deep mind of every person; there being available for healing and for help.[2]

In the Garden of Gethsemane, according to Mrs. Sanford, Jesus entered into a "deep rapport" with mankind. He "crashed" the collective unconscious of the human race and is therefore able to heal the hurts of the past:

> For now we know that we have within us another mind than the conscious, and that this unconscious mind is not disconnected from life but is connected

113

with the mind of the race: the collective unconscious.
. . . Now into this collective unconscious . . . Jesus
Christ entered, and there he lived during the days that
we rightly call Passion Week. He made a rapport in the
Garden of Gethsemane . . .with all people who ever
lived or ever will live upon the face of the earth. . . .
He became forever a part of the mass mind of the race,
so that even though His living being is now in heaven at
the right hand of the Father, a part of his consciousness
is forever bound up with the deep mind of man.[3]

Richard J. Foster in his very popular book *Celebration of
Discipline* (which charismatic leader Jamie Buckingham refers to
as a "classic for this generation")[4] teaches inner healing together
with other spiritual disciplines. Foster claims that he learned the
inner-healing prayer technique from Agnes Sanford. In describing the nature of the inner-healing prayer he writes:

The prayer is for the healing of inner wounds that the
sin has caused. . . . Invite God to flow into the deep
inner mind and heal the sorrows of the past. Picture the
healing. Thank Him for it.[5]

Foster finds another use for "picturing" or visualization. He
claims that through the imagination one enters the inner spiritual
world and is able to be catapulted into a "divine/human encounter." By visualizing a Bible story and becoming an active parti-
cipant, the event (according to Foster) becomes a present-tense
experience, since Jesus lives in the Eternal Now. He states:

. . . you can *actually* encounter the living Christ in
the event, be addressed by His voice and be touched by
His healing power. It can be more than an exercise of
the imagination; it can be a genuine confrontation.
Jesus Christ will actually come to you.[6]

The claim that man is able to encounter God by entering into
the inner world of the unconscious through meditative visualization is widely promoted in the writings of Episcopal priest

Morton Kelsey. In his book *Encounter with God* Kelsey explains how he was introduced to the reality that man is capable of directly encountering the divine.

> My own introduction to the idea that man can relate directly to the divine did not come to me through the work of any theologian. I first realized that this was not a dead issue through the work of a psychiatrist who was well versed in philosophical matters and deeply concerned with vital religion, Dr. Carl Jung.[7]

While it is true that Carl Jung never specifically stated that God existed within the unconscious mind, his writings certainly hinted at that reality. Jung claimed that the archetypes encountered in dreams and in active imagination possessed external objective reality in that they seemingly originated from outside the psyche, from the spiritual dimension. Kelsey states that Jung "discovered that images often bring contact with a world of psychic reality independent of the individual mind or personality."[8] Near the end of his life, Jung stated in an interview on the British Broadcasting Company, "Suddenly I understood that God was, for me at least, one of the most certain and immediate experiences . . . I do not believe; I know. I *know*.[9]

A QUICKER TRIP

If God exists within the unconscious mind, are there other ways and means besides meditative visualization by which we might reach Him and make contact?

In addition to the interpretation of dreams, hypnosis, journaling, and using a Ouija Board or tarot cards, there is a very interesting method which hastens this direct encounter with the "divine." Fifteen or twenty years ago Timothy Leary, a university professor, promoted the notion that the drug LSD had sacramental value in that it brought us to God. Leary's views may have been dismissed as preposterous some years ago, but today, in the light

of the "wisdom" revealed by inner-healing teachers and visualization advocates, his theories are becoming respectable.

According to research conducted by Stanislav Grof, the drug
LSD adds nothing to the human psyche but enables content from
the unconscious to be brought into the conscious. If God is to be
found within the unconscious, LSD becomes a quick trip to the
Almighty. Why waste time with visualization or dream interpretation when LSD does the same thing, only quicker and more
effectively? Grof discovered in researching over 2000 LSD-
induced experiments that many of the subjects claimed to have
been brought into the presence of God. The research by Grof also
confirmed the existence of womb-and-birth memories within the
unconscious mind, one of the intriguing doctrines of inner healing. But, sad to say, Grof's research also confirmed the "truth" of
reincarnation. [10]

Could it be true that God is able to be encountered within the
unconscious mind? Could dropping some LSD be a sacramental
trip? By meditating and visualizing could one actually be catapulted into a divine/human encounter? Does Jesus actually maintain a residence within the mass mind of the human race?

If such claims were indeed true, we are faced with the most
revolutionary discovery to be visited upon the Christian church
since the Reformation. The implications of this discovery would
be so great that we would be forced to undertake a total revision of
Christian theology. All these years we have thought that it was
necessary to hear the Word, partake of the biblical sacraments,
and be involved in the fellowship of the body of Christ in order to
develop our spiritual life. Now we discover that by popping a pill
or meditating our way into the unconscious we can carry on a
conversation with the real Jesus, hear His voice, and write down
in our journals the wisdom received in this personal interview.

COULD THE UNCONSCIOUS BE GOD HIMSELF?

But there is even greater "wisdom and truth" to be discovered
in the "religion of the unconscious." There are some inner-

healing teachers who actually believe that this mystical unconscious mind is not merely the container of God but is *God Himself*.
The September 1986 *Charisma* magazine published an article on
inner healing which was very illuminating. In that article David
Hazard spoke about what he called some of the "skeletons in the
inner healing closet":

> According to some, Eastern mysticism and even
> necromancy are infiltrating the movement in some
> quarters. "I know this is going to offend some people,
> says [Martin] Lynch cautiously, "but it has to be said.
> We're starting to see a deification of the unconscious.
> It's a major problem." Lynch, who is Roman Catholic,
> says that certain people "tend to be susceptible to the
> teachings of Carl Jung. But Jung is a nemesis. He's
> anti-Christian. He was a Gnostic and a purveyor of
> gnosticism."[11]

This is incredible! Some Christians are claiming to have finally
uncovered the divine hiding place! Contrary to what some of the
great philosophers of the past have thought, God was never
transcendent but merely unconscious. This incredible notion that
God Himself is the unconscious mind is certainly a radical depar-
ture from traditional, biblical Christianity.

The deification of the unconscious is not merely an isolated
heresy. The notion that God is the unconscious has been widely
promoted by M. Scott Peck in his book *The Road Less Traveled*,
read by well over one million people. A guide for group discussion, written by a Methodist minister, is also available. Peck
claims that Carl Jung did not go far enough:

> Jung never went quite so far as to actually state that
> God existed in the unconscious, although his writings
> clearly pointed in that direction. What he did do was
> to divide the unconscious into the more superficial,
> individual "personal unconscious" and the deeper

"collective unconscious" that is common to mankind. In my vision the collective unconscious is God; the conscious man is individual; and the personal unconscious is the interface between them. [12]

Peck describes his understanding of spiritual growth based upon unconscious spirituality by saying:

I have said that the ultimate goal of spiritual growth is for the individual to become as one with God. It is to know with God. Since the unconscious is God all along, we may further define the goal of spiritual growth to be the attainment of godhood by the conscious self. It is for the individual to become totally, wholly God. [13]

In the final analysis, according to Peck, man reaches the pinnacle of the evolutionary spiral. He becomes a new "life form of God."

WHAT IS AT STAKE?

Exposing the inner-healing/visualization teaching is not merely an exercise in picky apologetics or supercritical dogmatism. We are not dealing with a few little theological distortions that are of minor significance, but we are seeking to preserve the basic biblical understanding of the Christian faith.

The Christian church has always taught that God reaches down for man, rather than man reaching within for God. Revelation begins with God, and not with man "priming his visualization pump" to talk to Jesus. Biblical Christianity has always directed man outside himself to a God who, by the working of the Holy Spirit through the preaching of the Gospel acts upon man in order to bring him to faith and salvation. Christians believe that man is totally dependent upon the grace of God—grace which comes down from above and not up from within. God has reconciled us to Himself through the entrance of Jesus into this world. It is God who takes the initiative and gives repentance. It is God who works faith. It is God who saves and grants the new birth through the Holy Spirit. It is God who meets us in His Word and moves upon our hearts that we might abide each day in our relationship with the Lord Jesus Christ.

These facts are totally incompatible with the "religion of the unconscious" promoted by Carl Jung and his modern mystical disciples. Jung described his understanding of our relationship with God in this way:

> The Christian West considers man to be wholly dependent upon the Grace of God. . . . Grace comes from elsewhere, at all events from outside. Every other point of view is sheer heresy. Hence, it is quite understandable why the human psyche is suffering from undervaluation. Anyone who dares to establish a connection between the psyche and the idea of God is immediately accused of "psychologism" or suspected of morbid "mysticism." . . . We must get at the Eastern values from within and not from without, seeking them in ourselves, in the unconscious . . . we doubt the very thing that seems so obvious to the East, namely *the self-liberating power of the introverted mind.*[14]

At least Jung was correct in one point of his assessment: Grace does indeed come from outside. As he put it, "Every other point of view is sheer heresy."

THE MAZE OF DECEPTION

Even though the perverted understanding of the deification of the unconscious is not promoted by all inner-healing teachers, the deification of the unconscious is, according to Martin Lynch, a serious problem in the inner-healing movement. Visiting this nebulous concept of the unconscious mind upon the Christian church and using it to define spiritual experience produces an ever-increasing maze of deception and heresy. In spiritual matters there is always a progression; spiritual life is never stagnant: It is moving in either one direction or the other, into greater light or deeper darkness. If a person is walking in the light and living in the truth of the Gospel of Jesus Christ, there will be spiritual development. Truth leads to more truth, light to more light. The opposite is also true: Error and deception lead into deeper error and deception. It is for this reason that cults often have a way of self-destructing, ending in disaster. I predict that the same thing will take place in the inner-healing movement.

A teaching that may sound very good in the beginning may develop into blatant heresy, deception, and perversion if it does not have a solid foundation in Scripture. What starts out as an innocent, well-intentioned attempt to bring relief to people suffering from emotional wounds may well end up as a total redefinition of the Christian faith, creating something that is no longer identifiable with biblical understanding.

Without a basis in Scripture there is no way to correct a teaching. It will naturally progress as "revelation is added to revelation." To begin with an understanding of sanctification based upon the unconscious mind and to claim that Jesus wants to enter into the unconscious and heal it is to base a teaching on questionable theory. To go a step further and suggest that this unknown dimension of the unconscious is the spiritual dimension in which God is able to be discovered is, in the words of Viktor Frankl, "theological dilettantism"[15] or "theological trifling." To go the additional step and claim that this dimension of the unconscious is in fact God Himself is simply ludicrous.

Altered
Consciousness

10

Altered Consciousness

The technique of visualization that is used in the inner-healing ministry is associated with some rather weird theories. Many claims are made regarding the benefits of the technique in encountering spiritual reality or producing supernatural results. Let us consider some of the mechanics involved in visualization: how it is done and what it accomplishes.

RIGHT BRAIN/LEFT BRAIN

It is a generally accepted idea based on fairly sound research (especially conducted in the study of epilepsy) that the two sides of the brain control different functions. While the left side generally controls the thought/word/reason function of the human mind, the right side controls the visual/conceptual function. During normal thought process these two sides function interdependently, combining words, thoughts, and logical reasoning with imagination and conceptualization. For most people this mental function is somewhat unbalanced. While artists, authors, and visionary people in general are more "right-brain-oriented," mathematicians and logical objectivists are more "left-brain-oriented."

In order to engage in visualization, concentration must be directed at the pictures in the imagination. This requires a cessation of the left-brain function. Thoughts must be put to rest, and a passive mental state must be achieved. This practice, which is called "centering," may involve breathing exercises or "counting yourself down." The practice of "counting sheep" in order to go to sleep accomplishes the same result. One of the ladies in my Bible study group attended a weekend seminar on "centering prayer," involving visualization. As the leader counted the group down into a visualizing state of mind, she fell asleep.

ALPHA LEVEL

The research of German psychiatrist Hans Berger uncovered the nature of brain vibrations. In normal function, while the five senses are in use, the brain emits 13 to 18 vibrations per second. Below 8 vibrations per second a person falls asleep. Between 8 and 13 vibrations, visualization is able to take place. Vibrations at this frequency are called *alpha rhythms*. In his very popular book *Celebration of Discipline*, Richard Foster points out that meditative visualization, in addition to catapulting one into a divine/human encounter, maintains a consistent alpha-level brainwave pattern.[1]

The "alpha state" is associated with other interesting phenomena. The hypnotic trance exists within the alpha level. Because of this, the visualization technique is included within material offering self-hypnosis. The occult trances of an Edgar Cayce are found within alpha. A "truth serum" drug such as sodium Pentothal causes a person to lapse into the alpha state. If you are able to consciously observe, you will note that at the moment right before you fall asleep you will experience seemingly confused mental pictures. These are called *hypnagogic images* and occur as your relaxation passes through the alpha zone.

In order to initiate visualization, a state of "centered" relaxation requiring a passive mental process is necessary. A person is not able to concentrate upon the images in the imagination without being "centered." While some inner-healing teachers may claim that they do not use breathing exercises or other techniques to enter into the "visualization prayer," the issue is merely academic. If I instruct a person to relax, close his eyes, and visualize some event from the past, bringing the image of Jesus into the event, I am of necessity leading him down into alpha. While functioning at alpha level produces visualization, engaging in visualization will cause one to function at alpha.

DANGER?

Warnings regarding the dangers of the passive mental state which is used as a prelude for visualization have come forth from some of the saints of the past. The book *War on the Saints* by Jesse Penn-Lewis was written over 70 years ago. On the heels of the Pentecostal revival at the turn of the century appeared an outpouring of occultism, very similar to what we are experiencing today. Mrs. Penn-Lewis wrote her book for the purpose of providing a clear delineation between the work of the Holy Spirit and the work of demon spirits. I have found many of her distinctions to be somewhat helpful, especially to the subject at hand. Yet I believe that Penn-Lewis, in many of her distinctions, places too much emphasis on demon spirits and not enough emphasis on the sinful nature of men. We need to be careful in our definitions lest we discover demons behind every teapot. Note the distinction Mrs. Penn-Lewis makes between the working of the Holy Spirit and the operation of evil spirits.

> With all the various methods in vogue in the East and elsewhere, to bring about the manifestation and workings of supernatural powers . . . the principle is the same. The key to all these, and other Satanic workings in the human frame, is the need of the SUSPENSION OF MENTAL ACTIVITY; whereas in all Divine revelations, the mental faculties and powers are unchecked, and in full operation. . . . No supernatural "vision" in any form can be taken as of God which requires a CONDITION OF MENTAL NON-ACTION, or comes whilst the believer is in such a condition. . . . All the Holy Spirit's enlightening and illuminating vision is given when the mind is in full use, and every faculty awake to understand.[2]

A PRELUDE FOR PSYCHIC PHENOMENA

One of the fascinating elements associated with functioning at the passive alpha level is the alleged increase of the possibility of psychic phenomena taking place. This association of psychic phenomena with the "centering technique" certainly adds a whole new dimension to the maze of deception created by the visualization employed in inner healing.

Laurie and Tucker, whose book *Centering* is a mixture of occultism, Eastern mysticism, Christianity, and psychology, claim that achieving the meditative alpha state through breathing exercises and sense deprivation produces an expansion of awareness, heightening of present talents, and the discovery of new abilities. By continuing in meditation, they claim that a higher power can be contacted which includes PSI or ESP experiences.[3]

Mike and Nancy Samuels in their visualization textbook titled *Seeing with the Mind's Eye* point out:

> Researchers have found other evidence linking paranormal experiences with characteristics of both nonordinary consciousness and visualization. Paranormal experiences seem to be increased and strengthened by a relaxed state of body and mind, by faith in the phenomena, and by an expansive, imaginative frame of mind.[4]

In his "how to" book on meditation, Lawrence LeShan matter-of-factly states that paranormal experiences readily occur as one enters into the meditative altered state of consciousness. From his perspective, it is not surprising and should be expected.[5]

Jose Silva, the founder of Silva Mind Control, points out that in order to experience psychic phenomena, one must "put the logical mind in the back seat and the imaginative mind up front where the controls are." Silva claims that as imagination grows stronger, psychic powers increase: "It is the imaginative mind which holds them." From his perspective, operating at the alpha level enables a person to see both into the future and into the past.[6]

AGNES SANFORD'S MIND READING

Agnes Sanford, the founder of the inner-healing ministry, also speaks of psychic phenomena present in the practice of inner healing:

> But the actual deep therapy of the Holy Spirit is not done by us at all but by Him. And it is done by the union of two souls. It is not strange that we find ourselves knowing matters about a person's past that no one has ever told us. While the work is done by the Holy Spirit, the possibility of such instinctive knowing is already potentially within our natures. "Thought transfer-ence" it is called; the passing of thoughts from un-conscious to unconscious. This takes place all the time. Occasionally, when it would be helpful, the uncon-scious pushes up into the conscious mind as much as we need to know about a person. Thus in prayer for the healing of the memories, the Holy Spirit, working through us, quickens and enlivens a gift that is natural to us anyway. (In fact all the gifts of the Spirit are potentially within our natures.)[7]

Mrs. Sanford defines the relationship between the counselor and the counselee as the establishment of a "deep rapport." If you recall from the previous chapter, this same "deep rapport" through prayer was established between Jesus and all of mankind in the Garden of Gethsemane. Jesus entered into the "deep mind" of the human race by touching base with us in the collective unconscious.

In the inner-healing prayer, the counselor, based on the example of Jesus in the Garden, also enters into the same "deep rapport" with the counselee. This translates into "crashing" the uncon-scious mind of another person. In that "deep rapport" there is, according to Sanford, an exchange of thoughts from "soul to soul." She views the revelatory phenomena which allegedly exist in the inner-healing process as being of a natural and not a supernatural variety. She refers to it as *thought transference*, which the dictionary defines as mind reading. She claims that all of the gifts of the Spirit are potentially within our human nature.

Mrs. Sanford makes no distinction between occult psychic phenomena (such as mind reading, clairvoyance, and ESP) and the gifts of the Holy Spirit. In her understanding, the purpose of the Holy Spirit is to "quicken and enliven" our natural psychic abilities.

This understanding of the Holy Spirit quickening our natural gifts is generally believed by those who promote a Christian/occult syncretism. Edgar Cayce encouraged his disciples to "attune the deep springs of personhood" to the "Christ Spirit" in order to attain the highest levels of psychic ability.[8] In the occult explanations of Laurie and Tucker, the Pentecost experience of the disciples opened their "third eye," the visualization eye, enabling them to perform miracles. Laurie and Tucker speak of Agnes Sanford as an example of one who would tire herself out in psychic healing and needed the Holy Spirit to quicken and enliven her psychic ability.[9]

Howard Ervin of Oral Roberts University would not agree with Agnes Sanford's understanding of the gifts of the Holy Spirit. In his book *This Which Ye See and Hear* he points out that a clear distinction must be made between psychic phenomena and the legitimate manifestations of the Holy Spirit:

> Since the source of the Pentecostal experience is God, it is a spiritual rather than a mere psychic experience. By this we mean that it is an experience resulting from a vertical or supernatural relationship with God. By way of contrast, psychic or occult experiences lack this vertical dimension. They are a reflex of one's own unconscious mind interacting horizontally . . . with other personalities, either human or demonic.[10]

Ervin goes on to point out that even in the church psychic phenomena are confused with spiritual manifestations. Some people even erroneously claim, according to Ervin, that extrasensory manifestations are valid expressions of the Holy Spirit's activity. The position expressed by Howard Ervin has been generally accepted as truth within much of Christianity.

OCCULTISM?

In spite of the fact that inner-healing teachers claim that the Holy Spirit gives supernatural insight and visions and that the gifts of the Holy Spirit are present in the inner-healing ministry, the words of Agnes Sanford and the claims associated with the use of "centered" visualization seem to demonstrate otherwise. The inner-healing technique promotes a psychic/spiritual confusion.

In his book *The Latent Power of the Soul* (written over 50 years ago), Watchman Nee, a Chinese evangelist who spent the last years of his life imprisoned for his faith, speaks of the intentions and strategy of the devil. According to his understanding, the attempt to interpret Christian spiritual experience in terms of psychological concepts is a massive deception of the devil. Nee explains:

> Throughout these thousands of years, Satan has been exerting himself to influence men into expressing their latent power. . . . This is his singular purpose which he has been cultivating. . . . He will confuse God's miracles. He wishes mankind to believe that all miracles in the Bible are but psychological in their origin, thus lowering their value. He wants men to think that they are able to do whatever the Lord Jesus did.[11]

This confusion between psychic phenomena and the supernatural manifestations of the Holy Spirit is readily discerned in the writings of Agnes Sanford and others who promote the visualization technique. For example, in his book *Transcend*, Jungian advocate Morton Kelsey gives us his understanding of paranormal phenomena and the place of these psychic or psi experiences within Christianity. He writes:

> The paranormal is understood as natural and morally neutral and may be used for either good or evil. Thus psi experiences can be used to point the way to an understanding of classical Christianity and help modern Christians grasp the power of that Christianity and share in it.

Kelsey goes on to point out that the Bible is a mine of information on these *natural and neutral* psi phenomena. According to his understanding, the Old Testament condemnation of psychic phenomena is not shared by the New Testament. Our Lord Jesus, according to Kelsey, practiced clairvoyance and mind reading and passed on these powers to His disciples.[12]

ALTERED STATES

In evaluating the claims concerning the altered state of consciousness achieved in the visualization technique, clear thinking is very important. I operate on the general position that the cause of distortion, deception, occultism, and involvement with evil spirits exists in *the hearts of people* rather than in methods, movements, techniques, and "isms." For example, I am not against the field of psychology and do not view it as a threat to the Christian faith. I find some value in psychology, but not for sanctification or holiness. My daughter is pursuing her degree in "Child Study." Of necessity, her studies involve a great deal of psychology. The insights offered by psychology in understanding retardation or even the psychology of the exceptional child are very helpful. But also recognize that there are many perverted psychologists who offer distorted views which are contrary to our biblical understanding. Being against psychology because there are perverted psychologists is comparable to being against biology because there are evolutionists, or being against sociology because there are communists. Let us not respond to deception hysterically. We need to locate problems where they exist: in the hearts and minds of people, and not in techniques or movements or academic disciplines.

As we have seen Christian visualization advocates, by employing Jungian psychology, claim that the altered state of consciousness achieved in the visualization technique (the passive "centered" mental state) causes a person to enter the spiritual dimension in which both good and evil content can be confronted. Within this nebulous dimension they are seeking that which is good. They believe that the image of Jesus envisioned is the real Jesus.

On the other hand, Christians who believe that the visualization technique is an occult technique claim that the altered state of consciousness produced in visualization taps into the demonic dimension. According to Jesse Penn-Lewis, it is a natural precondition for the operation of demons.

From my perspective, after studying this subject in great detail and spending much time seeking the Lord for wisdom, I do not accept the idea that the altered state of consciousness achieved in visualization *taps into any dimension whatever, whether divine or demonic or a mixture of both.* I do not believe that the altered state is a natural prelude for contacting any spiritual entities, whether good or evil.

Obviously the Bible does not indicate that an altered state of consciousness is a necessary condition for being "in the Spirit." To claim that centering down to alpha-level brain waves is a natural precondition for experiencing the reality of the Holy Spirit or for conducting a visual interview with the Lord Jesus is ludicrous. *Man does not set the conditions for encountering God.* Such thinking is totally out of line with the content of Scripture. The apostle Paul says in Romans 11:36: "From him and through him and to him are all things. To him be glory forever. Amen." Our relationship with the Lord Jesus is not dependent upon some physical adjustment in our brain waves. An oscilloscope cannot be used to measure spirituality.

On the other hand, I believe it is just as unreasonable to suggest that the alpha-level state of altered consciousness, in and of itself, opens the individual to the demonic dimension and demonic control. Promoting this notion is to believe that every night before going to sleep or every morning before awakening we pass through a demon dimension. Such is highly unlikely. I sincerely doubt that "counting sheep" in order to go to sleep brings the devil on the scene. If a person sits back in his easy chair, listens to soothing music, and visualizes some serene outdoor scene, he will attain the alpha state. This is called "relaxation therapy." I have difficulty suggesting that such a technique used to induce relaxation is evil *in and of itself*. I know a young woman who is a physical therapist and is often called upon to work with children who are nervous and "hyper." She uses the visualization technique to produce relaxation in the children. Is this an occult technique that taps into a demon dimension, or is it merely a human reality, a fact of physiology? It is one thing to say that the technique is occult; it is something different to say that *occultists use the technique*.

MISDIRECTED PEOPLE

If a person willfully seeks to create that "centered" alpha-level altered state of consciousness for the express purpose of engaging psychic phenomena and believes that spiritual reality and supernatural power can be discovered while in that condition, we are dealing with something totally different. The individual himself is seeking a spiritual dimension and contact with God. I am sure that the devil is very happy to oblige and create the experience. The error, as I see it, is not in the "centered state of mind" itself. The error is in the heart and mind of the person who has the erroneous, distorted notion that God can be contacted by altering consciousness and that the "real Jesus" appears in visualization. If I go out looking for God in places and in experiences where He has not promised to be found, I am inviting demonic delusion. If I believed that in jogging I could find Jesus and defined the "jogger's high" as being a spiritual experience, I am sure the devil would confirm my delusion. The problem is not in the jogging, but in the deluded jogger! Such applies to Ouija Boards, astrology, or seeking divine guidance in a fortune cookie.

The deception is not in the *technique* but in the *misguided people* who use the technique and claim to find Jesus. If I would say to you, "Do you know that by relaxing and lowering your brain waves to 8-13 vibrations per second you can form mental pictures, envision the real Lord Jesus Christ, and talk to Him?" how should you respond? If you had a decent working knowledge of Scripture and an ounce of common sense, you would smile, shake your head, and walk away.

Pastor Mark Virkler, a member of the Assemblies of God, believes that the silent, passive mental state achieved by "centering" causes a person to enter the dimension of "spirit impressions." He promotes the technique in his book *Dialogue With God* and offers his readers a cassette tape which teaches the technique for establishing the "centered" state of mind.

Virkler attempts to prove his position from Scripture, claiming that he uses the "Berean method" of Bible study. The primary verse of Scripture used by Virkler to develop his scenario is Habakkuk 2:1: "I will take my stand to watch, and station myself on the tower, and look forth to see what he will say to me. . . ."

In that single verse of Scripture Virkler discovers "centering," visualization, and dialogue with God! When the prophet "took his stand to watch" he was, according to Virkler, entering into "centering" silence. "Looking forth to see" means visualization. What God spoke to the prophet was through inner dialogue. In verse 2 God instructs the prophet to write down the vision. From Virkler's perspective, that means journaling the divine interview.[13]

Edmond Jacobs in his *Theology of the Old Testament* suggests another interpretation. From his understanding, the Old Testament prophets were not mystics. They functioned as Jesse Penn-

Lewis stated, with "the mind in full use, and every faculty awake to understand." Jacobs writes:

> When a prophet is called he is not found in a state of semi-consciousness; on the contrary, his sensitiveness is heightened rather: with eyes fully open to the outside world, the prophet takes as the starting point of his vision real objects which come before his sensitive perception. Thus Jeremiah's almond branch (1:11) and Amos's basket of fruits (8:1ff) are not set before a visionary gaze, but before normal perception; but the particular bond of knowledge, which at that moment unites the prophet to his God, charges these objects with deeper content.[14]

When the prophet Habakkuk ascended the tower and looked forth among the peoples below to see what the Lord would say to him, he saw many perversions among God's people. Read the rest of the chapter and you will see what he saw. It is the "vision" which he recorded, a vision which began with the real events probably occurring in the marketplace below.

Virkler's attempt to prove the technique of centering and visualization on the basis of Scripture is a futile exercise. It simply cannot be done.

Counterfeit Fruit

11

Counterfeit Fruit

While it is true that the concept of inner healing is based upon some very suspicious theories, and while it is true that the inner-healing methodology is delusion, yet the results of the inner-healing ministry in the lives of people often seem to be quite positive. I have no reason to question the truthfulness of the many people who claim to have been helped by inner healing. On the other hand, neither do I have any reason to deny the claim of Carl Jung that one-third of his patients were healed and another third showed improvement.[1]

The question we are dealing with in this chapter is whether we discern truth on the basis of results. Is it possible to produce seemingly good results by methods that are totally out of line with God's way of doing things? Are methods as important as results?

TESTING THE FRUIT

In his review of *The Seduction of Christianity*, Peter Davids raises the following criticism of the conclusions made by Dave Hunt:

> *The Seduction of Christianity* fails to test the fruit of the teachings and movements it criticizes. For example, it labels inner healing as sorcery which opens the mind to demonic guides. We know what happens when people play with the occult—they subject themselves to demonic influences. But, in most cases, after inner healing, people regularly want to pray more, love God more, love others more, read their Bibles more. Is this the fruit of the devil?[2]

Peter Davids' point is well taken: We cannot ignore the fruit of a movement. But are personal results the only fruit that we must evaluate? What about the fruit of truth? Is there theological fruit that must also be discerned? In fact, is not theological "truth fruit" more important than personal-results fruit?

The inner-healing methodology is part of a larger movement in which psychological technique is being used to produce seemingly supernatural, spiritual results. This creates many problems for the church in terms of discernment. We have normally thought that the "fruit of the Spirit" was not able to be counterfeited. Where you discovered apparent love, peace, and joy you had legitimate Christianity. In the light of the offerings of some people within the field of psychology, this position must be reconsidered.

Pragmatist philosopher and psychiatrist William James in his 1902 classic *The Varieties of Religious Experience* expressed a view on the subject of religious experience which characterizes the attitude that many people have taken toward inner healing and Jungian mysticism:

> In the history of Christian mysticism the problem how to discriminate between such messages and experiences as were really divine miracles, and such others as the demon in his malice was able to counterfeit . . . has always been a difficult one to solve, needing all the sagacity and experience of the best directors of conscience. In the end it had to come to our empiricist criterion: By their fruits ye shall know them, not by their roots. . . . You must all be ready now to judge the religious life by its results exclusively, and I will assume that the bugaboo of morbid origin will scandalize your piety no more.[3]

The belief that truth is discerned on the basis of results is called *pragmatism*. Robert Wise points out in *The Church Divided* that Agnes Sanford was pragmatic: She was more concerned with results than with theological definition.[4] On The John Ankerberg

Show, Jose Silva (the founder of Silva Mind Control) made his position very clear. He believes that the only criterion for judging the experience of "inner spirit guides" is results. Where the experience originates is not important.

William James quoted from the autobiography of famous sixteenth-century mystic Saint Theresa of Avila, who suggested the same criterion of discernment.

> A genuine heavenly vision yields a harvest of ineffable spiritual riches, and an admirable renewal of bodily strength. I alleged these reasons to those who so often accused my visions of being the work of the enemy of mankind and the sport of my imagination. . . . I showed them the jewels the divine hand had left with me. All those who knew me saw that I was changed. . . . As for myself, it was impossible to believe that if the demon were its author, he could have used, in order to lose me and lead me to hell, an expedient so contrary to his own interests as that of uprooting my vices and filling me with masculine courage and other virtues instead.[5]

In discerning the visions of Saint Theresa there are other ingredients which must come into play. For example, James points out that Saint Theresa hated Lutherans and longed for their overthrow. In one of her mystical "visions" she received supernatural insight into the manner in which the Mother of God was assumed into the Godhead.[6]

How would such a mystical vision be discerned? Would we employ the mere pragmatic criteria suggested by Saint Theresa herself, or would we also employ theological and biblical standards of discernment? Would we "judge by truth"? I would certainly hope so.

In the light of what psychologists are offering and suggesting, pragmatic discernment simply does not work. When it comes to the results offered in the inner-healing ministry, we must ask the question, *Is the devil willing to trade healing for heresy, deliverance for deception, emotional health for doctrinal confusion?* I believe he is.

WHAT AND HOW

Biblical truth is a combination of *concepts* and *directions*. I like to think of it as "what" and "how." God did not only tell us *what* He wants, but He also told us *how* He wants it. If you take the correct "what" and add the wrong "how" you produce heresy, deception, and all kinds of confusion. The heresy of legalism, for example, is doing what God wants according to wrong methods. While God desires righteousness in our lives, it is not to be accomplished by rigidly following a list of rules, even though the self-disciplined person might attain some degree of success. In Romans 10:1-3 the apostle Paul bemoans the condition of Israel. While Israel has a zeal for God, it is not an enlightened zeal. They try to establish their own righteousness rather than submitting to the manner in which God makes man righteous in Christ Jesus. They are doing the right thing in the wrong way. He who does *the right thing in the wrong way* is just as disobedient as he who simply does *the wrong thing*.

I believe that the devil works more intently at methods than doctrines. Within the life of the church, doctrines are usually established and creeds are confessed, but methods are often discerned by results. It is not easy to sneak a false doctrine into a confessional church, but the introduction of wrong methods, especially if they seemingly produce good results, usually goes by unnoticed. Human nature is geared more to results than to methods: "The end justifies the means." All one has to do is examine some of the fund-raising techniques employed in many doctrinally solid churches to discover the truth of this principle.

If you analyze the wilderness temptations of our Lord Jesus, you will note that in each case the *method* rather than the truth was being attacked.

In the first instance, after fasting for 40 days, Jesus hungered. This presented no real problem to our Lord, since He was able to miraculously turn water into wine and feed 5000 people. The devil said, "Command the stones to become bread." There was nothing wrong with turning stones into bread; no commandment or moral law or point of theology was being violated. Yet if Jesus had turned the stones into bread He would have been using His divine power to meet His own personal needs. In essence He would have been "commanding His blessings."

In the second instance, by tempting Jesus to jump from the pinnacle of the temple the devil was offering "instant messiah-ship." He even gave Jesus a verse to "claim and stand upon." Yet Jesus knew that it is always wrong to tempt God, no matter how wonderful the results may be.

In the third temptation, the result would have been the attainment of the kingdoms of this world if Jesus would merely bow before the devil. Jesus knew that "the kingdoms of this world would become the kingdoms of our God and of His Christ," but the divine method was through the cross and resurrection. The devil offered to Jesus the shortcut to attaining the same results.

In comparing these temptations to the conditions existing in the church today, it seems to me that the devil does not have an original thought in his mind. In the "prosperity teaching" we are offered the same temptation: to speak the word and create our own blessings. In other teachings many people are led to throw away medication, to take the risk of faith, to stand upon the Word and test the promises of God. Finally, a questionable technique borrowed from the occult is being offered to help establish "the kingdom within."

In assessing the conditions that exist in the world and in the church, many Christians wring their hands and become anxious. "God," they ask, "how are You ever going to accomplish Your purposes?" God has revealed to us the outcome. The victory is ours. The kingdom will be established. The body of Christ will become the bride of Christ. God has all things under control. But in spite of knowing the end result we do not have clear insight into the ways and means which the Father will use to produce this result. If we are not willing to wait in patience for God to accomplish His purposes by using His methods, the devil stands ready to offer shortcuts to seemingly produce the same divinely intended results.

It seems to me that many Christians have "fallen in the wilderness."

If you apply the "what" and "how" analysis to the inner-healing ministry you might arrive at the conclusion, after reading the testimonies, that the ministry seemingly accomplishes "what" God desires: happy, burden-free, emotionally healthy people. But what about the "how"? It is here that the questions must be raised. The motives may be right, but the methods are wrong.

PSYCHOLOGICAL COUNTERFEIT

There is experiential content in psychological techniques which appears to counterfeit the blessings to be found in Christ and applied by biblical methodology. For example, we know that God wants a church made up of people who love each other—who are concerned and empathetic and who reach out and touch other people with the love of God. God wants His people joined together and unified. This is *what* He wants. But *how* will we accomplish that desire on the part of the Father?

Nearly 20 years ago I participated in an intense sensitivity or encounter experience. The congregation I was serving in Michigan had called a female church worker to become part of our staff. It seemed that in the past, many of the young women who had prepared for full-time service in our church's deaconess program had encountered some relational problems with the pastors of the congregations in which they were called to serve. The administrators of the program decided to put together that year's graduating class with the pastors with whom they would be serving in marathon sensitivity or encounter groups, hoping that through the experience they would get along better. So one day I traveled to Valparaiso University in Valparaiso, Indiana, to attend what I thought was a conference with the deaconess graduating class. I had absolutely no idea what I was about to encounter.

When I arrived at the gathering, we were divided up into three mixed groups. I was in a group of four pastors and seven young women. We met in the basement lounge. As we came together, the leader of the group, a professional "facilitator," announced, "This is your group. Do with it as you please." At that he sat back, puffed on his pipe, and smiled like a Cheshire cat.

CRACKING THE HUSK

We gathered together as a group for 24 hours spread out over $2\frac{1}{2}$ days. The encounter dynamic that took place in that group was incredible. "Guts were spilled," insecurities unmasked, exterior husks cracked open. Each person had the privilege of being "picked at" by the group. At the conclusion we gathered together with arms around each other expressing our love and concern. With a young woman seated upon his lap, the facilitator expressed the ideal, "Wouldn't it be wonderful if the entire church could experience what we have experienced these past days?"

I had been involved in a "deep rapport," a "soul-sharing" encounter with a group of Christian people. I went home a totally different person. Morton Kelsey accurately defines the husk-breaking experience as "being a rebirth into a new dimension."[7] The founder of the encounter group movement, Carl Rogers, describes the result of an encounter experience as being a "new birth."[8] Upon entering the house, I greeted my wife. Looking straight into her eyes, I expressed the fact that I loved her and confessed that I had not been the kind of loving, concerned husband that I should have been.

My life and ministry were adjusted. I dressed differently, no longer in basic black. I let my hair grow and learned how to play the guitar. Love, joy, and peace were the themes of my life. My preaching changed drastically. Love was the keynote. I taught that God's people had to come to a place of openness with each other, sharing real needs, taking off the masks, and expressing the love that is within. God's desire, so I thought, was to crack the human husk, the thick insecure flesh that would not allow the gentle love of Jesus to come through. Previously I had greeted my people at the door with my right hand as I held my hymnal in my left. No longer did I hold the hymnal. Now I wanted to reach out and touch, to be warm, open, and loving to my people.

Every group that I was a part of, from Sunday school teachers to confirmation class, became encounter groups. I encouraged people to be open with each other, to take off the masks and be real, expressing the genuine desires of their hearts.

DISCOVERING NEW TRUTH

I became a highly reflective person. I was experiencing a new level of consciousness. New thoughts and ideas would bombard my mind. For hours I could sit quietly and entertain the thoughts that entered in. I welcomed them. As a result of such "revelation," I came to the conclusion that the greatest hindrance to God's people being open and honest with each other was the innate fear of sexuality. A man and a woman will not hug each other, I reasoned, because they are afraid of where it will lead. Therefore, somehow that fear of our own sexuality must be overcome if the church is to be the committed, unified body of people that God intends it to be.

New ideas defining the basic truths of Christianity in sexual constructs came out of nowhere. The revelatory experience was highly charged with psychic energy. I was enlightened to see that the Old Testament clearly taught that God and Israel were in a marriage relationship. I found the theme throughout the prophets, especially in Hosea. I determined that God's entrance into Israel through Christ was a penetrating sexual act. Through that copulative act, climaxed on Good Friday, the seed of the

Spirit was implanted into the womb of Israel, bringing forth a new creation, people who were born "not of the flesh, not of the will of men, but of God." Peter declared that we were born again by a living and imperishable seed (1 Peter 1:23). I looked up that verse in the Greek and discovered that the word "seed" was the Greek word *sperma*.

Everything I had discovered by revelation I was able to read into the Bible. I shared my views with anyone who would listen. Of course, if they did not accept my ideas, it was their problem: They too had a fear of their own sexuality. I corresponded with one of my seminary professors, sharing my insights. I sincerely believed that I had discovered truth which would change the course of the church. I was enmeshed in this deception for nearly two years.

DELIVERANCE

But God in His grace did not leave me alone. One day a man by the name of Russ Cooper came to my door. He claimed to be selling certain motivational products, but told me later that the Lord had sent him to share the reality of Jesus with me. Russ showed me from the New Testament that there was nothing good in me; everything was in Christ Jesus. The Word that he shared, according to the promises of God, worked within my heart. A few months later I began to attend a Charismatic prayer meeting, and Jesus baptized me in the Holy Spirit. The Holy Spirit opened my eyes to the depth of deception in which I had been living. I wrote letters to those with whom I had shared my "new truth," apologizing for being so dumb. I came to the conclusion that a deceived person can find anything he wants to in Scripture.

Deception is a horrible experience. At the time you are involved, you experience great inflation, thinking that you see something new that others before you have not seen. You search Scripture and amazingly find biblical support for your deception. You believe that for some unknown reason God has placed His hand upon you to reveal the truth to the world. But when you get out of the deception and look back, you feel like a fool. I honestly feel sorry for people who believe that Jungianism provides the light through which Scripture is to be viewed. I empathize with people who actually believe that they can encounter God by altering their state of consciousness. For some of these people it will be very difficult to get out of the deception, especially if they have written books publicly promoting their new insights. There is a pride factor involved. It is very difficult to say, "I was wrong!"

RIGHTLY DIVIDING

As a result of these two experiences, one psychic and the other spiritual, my teaching within the church was greatly influenced. I taught the following distinction long before I knew anything about Jung, visualization, or inner healing. There are two kinds of experience which seemingly produce similar results and must be distinguished to avoid deception.

There are two types of wisdom (James 3:15-17): that which comes down from above and that which comes up from within. Divine insight comes down from above as we actively reach out, with our senses alive and alert, in praise, worship, and thanksgiving unto Jesus, who is truly worthy of our praise. But there is another wisdom that comes up from within. The Bible speaks of it as earthly, psychic, and demonic. It is the wisdom received by Carl Jung, Agnes Sanford, and visualization teachers who seek to find God within their own inner world, claiming that a personal interview and dialogue can be conducted with the visualized Jesus. Such reception requires a "centered" state of mind. The wisdom from above comes down in the midst of the praises of God's people and in their active involvement, with all senses alive and alert, in His Word.

There are two types of relationships. Encounter forms "soul-to-soul" relationships. These are energy-charged relationships, produced by individuals opening themselves to other individuals. As a result of my dual experience, I have taught prayer and praise groups to never become "spill-your-guts-and-let's-be-real" groups. The dynamic in such relationships is very real and tangible, but it is also a deceptive counterfeit. Relationships in the body of Christ are formed as a result of people *getting closer to Jesus*. He is the "hub" and we are the "spokes." As we are drawn closer to the Lord Jesus, we are automatically drawn closer to each other. You do not develop good relationships in the body of Christ by teaching about the dynamic of relationships. You get good relationships by teaching people to abide in Christ Jesus.

There are two kinds of fruit. Christians who believe that the devil cannot counterfeit the fruit of the Spirit are foolish. I know a woman who works in the counseling center of a large university. She interacts each day with psychologists and counselors. She recently said to me, "These people are the most kind, empathetic, loving people I have ever met, but most of them are atheists." There is a genuine release of love and compassion in "soul-to-soul" relationships. But it is a counterfeit. The fruit of the Spirit is not found in a "soul-to-soul deep rapport" with other people, but in our being drawn into a closer walk with Jesus.

I have never met face-to-face with those who advocate Jungian psychology and inner journeys. I imagine these people are some of the kindest, sweetest, most loving people you can find. If you look at some of the pictures of Carl Jung in his old age, he appears to have been a beautiful man. When you read his heretical writings you expect to behold some horned creature, not some Santa Claus type with a bright smile and twinkling eyes, the kind of man with whom you would love to spend an evening discussing "spiritual matters."

I can also understand the appeal of psychic experience. There is something very real, exciting, and numinous about the content that comes up from within. Thinking back to 20 years ago, I would have been a viable candidate for meditation and visualization. Sitting on the patio on a summer evening with my eyes closed and allowing all kinds of energy-charged thoughts to flow through my mind was a highly pleasurable, exciting, invigorating experience. I do not deny the reality of the experience, nor do I deny the reality of the fruit of personal character resulting from the experience.

THE FRUIT OF TRUTH

But let us apply to inner healing and visualization the standard of the *fruit of truth* and see what happens.

It is interesting to observe that everyone who alters his consciousness and enters into the inner world of this unconscious dimension comes out wanting to redefine Christianity. Carl Jung did not seem to have an orthodox thought in his head. All his religious concepts were directed toward a new understanding of the Christian faith, viewed through the grid of Eastern mysticism, occult alchemy, and heretical gnosticism. Morton Kelsey seeks to redefine Christianity as psychology. M. Scott Peck in his work *What Return Can I Make?* offers his own understanding of the Christian faith:

> Whatever the final results of the right brain/left brain research may prove to be—whether male/female differences are more sociological than biological— there does seem to be a feminine quality to the gift of wisdom, as well as a feminine receptivity to that gift. I myself think of the Holy Spirit as predominantly feminine.[9]

Throughout his book he refers to the Holy Spirit as "she."

Those who teach the visualization method suggest a new use of Scripture. Rather than using the stories and parables in the New Testament as the basis for discovering truth and the principles of God's working, they are now being used as an arena for visualization. Visualizers jump into the stories and claim to talk to Jesus. Books are available giving the Jungian interpretation of the Gospels.

In the beginning of this chapter I quoted Peter David's claim that those who receive inner healing "pray more, love God more, love others more, read their Bibles more." While this may be true, the problem is that through "visualization prayer" each of these elements can be redefined in terms of a mystical devotion or discipline. In fact, "pray more, love God more, love others more, and read their Bibles more" really proves very little. Edgar Cayce taught a Bible class for 24 years and was a man of prayer who possessed a deep devotion for God and love toward his fellow-man. This certainly does not make his experiences any less occult.

After all is said and done, the only secure objective source of discernment remains the written Word of God. It is here that our discussion of inner healing and visualization began. It is here that it must end.

Back to Scripture

12

Back to Scripture

It is critically important that we place inner healing in the proper perspective from the vantage points of both Christian doctrine and church history. By doing so we will accurately identify the root of the problem and in the future avoid further pitfalls of deception. Understanding the historical perspective of visualization as it appears in ancient mysticism will temper our response to this teaching and guard against a simplistic overreaction.

A NEW EMPHASIS

God's people can easily get caught up in this present deception because the inner-healing teachers and visualization advocates claim to be orthodox, Bible-believing Christians. In opposing the inner-healing/visualization movement, we are not encountering the denial of basic Christian doctrines. The conflict is not the same as that created by the various cults, who deny the trinity or reject the deity of the Lord Jesus Christ. Advocates of inner healing and visualization claim that they believe in the inspiration and inerrancy of Scripture and confess the historic creeds of the church.

In dealing with the inner-healing/visualization movement we encounter a paradigm shift, a different way of looking at the same truth, rather than a denial of the truth itself. Such truths as sanctification, prayer, "seeing Jesus through the eyes of faith," "being changed into the image of Jesus," or "being confronted with the person of Jesus Christ" become open to completely new explanations and interpretations. The biblical command to "look unto Jesus," previously defined as setting our affections above, where Jesus is seated at the right hand of God, now assumes the interpretation of seeing Jesus through introverted contemplation and visualization. Some even suggest that "being changed into the image of Jesus" means "being changed into the Jesus we image." Mark Virkler publishes a computer readout of all verses in Scripture pertaining to "looking" or "seeing" and interprets them to mean visualization. The verses for the most part mean nothing more than the physical act of looking and seeing. Virkler claims that this is the "Berean method" of doing Scripture study.[1]

SCRIPTURE INTERPRETS SCRIPTURE

To guard against the deception created by such an emphasis which changes the meaning and interpretation of basic biblical truth, Christians must become more sensitive to well-proven biblical interpretation which leads to sound theology. By "well-proven biblical interpretation" I mean principles of interpretation that have been established throughout the history of the church to protect the people of God from deception and heresy.

The primary principle in *hermeneutics* or biblical interpretation is that *Scripture interprets Scripture*. This principle was developed at the time of the Reformation to combat the special place which the Roman Catholic Church had assumed as the interpreters of Scripture. While Catholic Church leaders claimed to be the interpreters of Scripture for the people, the Protestant Reformers declared that Scripture interprets itself, or *what comes from Scripture is interpreted by Scripture*.

The *Scripture interprets Scripture* principle protects the church from well-intentioned people who begin with concepts borrowed from outside sources, such as psychology, Eastern religions, or even occultism, and seek to prove that such concepts are valid for Christians by appealing to specific Bible verses which are given a new interpretation. The principle means that you cannot interpret the Bible *in the light of mysticism or Jungian psychology*. You cannot define biblical truths on the basis of some nebulous concept of the unconscious mind and still retain orthodox

Christianity. It cannot be done! You can only interpret the Bible *in the light of the Bible*.

If you approach the Word with the understanding that Scripture interprets Scripture, you cannot throw a "curve ball" that does not fit into the total theme of the revealed Word of God. This vital principle refutes those who find some verses in the Bible which seem to confirm their notions and then proceed to build their entire system upon them, regardless of whether their new twists fit into the theological framework of Scripture.

If this principle of Reformation were followed by Protestant Christians today, we would not have such confusion within the church. The problem is that when some pastors "get the Holy Ghost" they throw out legitimate hermeneutics and interpret Scripture "by the seat of their pants." You cannot replace sound exegesis with "The Lord showed me" or eradicate the foundation of the authority of Scripture by claiming that "truth is truth."

THE IMPORTANCE OF SOUND DOCTRINE

Systematic doctrinal theology which governs the teaching of the church and defines the "what" and "how" of our relationship with the Lord Jesus Christ is drawn from Scripture by using sound principles of interpretation. Many charismatics have naively reacted against doctrine, claiming that a relationship with the Lord Jesus and the experience of the Holy Spirit replaces sound doctrine. *This is never the case.* Doctrine which is legitimately drawn from Scripture defines and describes the relationship we enjoy with the Lord Jesus and provides a sound framework for us to live out our faith.

Doctrines drawn from the inspired Word of God form a unified, integrated whole. All the various elements, such as the understanding of sin and repentance, of justification and sanctification, and of the forgiveness of sins and the new birth, fit and work together. Loose theological ends have to be interpreted in the light of the total theological picture. Sometimes even a small distortion in one element of theology may change the entire system.

A number of years ago I became friends with a man who was pastoring a small discipleship fellowship. While we both believed in the reality of the power of the Holy Spirit and the supernatural gifts of the Spirit, our fellowships functioned in a totally different manner. The people in my congregation were actively stepping out in the pursuit of ministry while his people were sitting back and waiting for God to do something in their midst. He thought that my people were functioning "in the flesh," but I thought that his people were just spiritually stagnant.

One day we sat down for an afternoon and discussed our differences. Eventually our difference came down to the basic concept of the nature of man. I believed and taught, according to the doctrinal position of my church, that man had been corrupt-ED by sin. Man's will, intellect, and emotions, though corrupt-ED, were still redeemable and renewable. He taught, on the other hand, that man was CORRUPT. His will, intellect, and emotions were not usable and were identified with the sinful flesh. Our differences were no greater than the letters -ED. But the results were dramatic. While my people functioned together and moved out into various ministries, his people waited for God to do something. God never "moved." The people became disillusioned and discouraged, and finally disbanded.

With this in mind, it is important to understand that the concept taught by inner-healing teachers that "the real Jesus is able to be encountered in visualization" cannot be introduced as a new truth without distorting and redefining the basic theology of the church. This "visualization claim" is not just a minor point of theology; *it adjusts the entire understanding of how Jesus comes to us today.* The theological principles of the Reformation are that Jesus comes to us by the *grace of God alone* (without priming the visualization pump), through *faith alone* (and not by sight), working through *Scripture alone* as the means by which God's grace in Christ Jesus is offered (and not by a direct encounter with the living Christ in our imagination). To claim that the real Jesus of history can be directly encountered in visualization is contrary to Protestant theology and will potentially distort the substance of the Christian faith. The basic truth that Jesus is offered to people *only* through the preaching of the Gospel is being questioned.

It is very important for God's people to develop an eye for the erroneous use of Scripture and a sensitivity to sound doctrine. When you hear or read a concept which is being offered as a legitimate Christian truth, ask yourself the question: *Does the concept come out of Scripture as a part of the total theme of God's Word or is it being read into Scripture?* Did the person offering the concept find it in the Bible, or did he find it elsewhere and then try to prove it from the Bible? I would challenge you to read the biblical support given in behalf of inner healing or visualization with these principles in mind and see what you discover.

ORTHODOX CHRISTIANITY?

Those who engage in the practice of visualization as a means of producing inner healing or positive spiritual growth claim that they retain the basic doctrines of the church and should be regarded as orthodox Christians. If this claim were true, I would be more than happy to dismiss the issue and regard "visualization prayer" as just a preference of personal piety, placing it in the same category as praying with your hands folded or praying with your arms raised.

But the fact is that those who claim that Jesus is able to be encountered in visualization are far from being orthodox Christians. Putting it very simply, they are promoting heretical teaching which cannot be integrated into the basic doctrines of the Christian faith.

The problem goes beyond disagreement in principle and doctrine. Those who practice meditative visualization are engaged in communication with an imaged figure who they claim is the real Lord Jesus Christ. They talk to this figure, receive guidance from this figure, and have "unconscious wounds" healed by this figure. Worse yet, if we are dealing with a demonic counterfeit, they lead other people into the same experience, introducing them to the method by which they too can have their own "imaged figure of Jesus." Is this orthodox Christianity?

The problem that exists within the charismatic movement today cannot be blamed primarily on the philosophy of Carl Jung or the teachings of Agnes Sanford. Neither Jung nor Sanford are with us today. The problem is that there are leaders in the charismatic movement who have little concern for biblical doctrine or for proper methods of interpreting Scripture. When confronted with deceptive teaching based on shabby interpretations, they are not willing to publicly refute the error, but instead claim that God will take care of the problem. Many shepherds seem to be far more interested in defending their friends than in protecting their sheep from heresy. If there is inadequate desire or means within the charismatic movement for correcting doctrine and for warning the sheep of dangerous teachings, the movement will always be in the grips of deception.

THE HISTORICAL PERSPECTIVE

Past history has a way of putting present experience into the proper perspective. By demonstrating to us that there is really "nothing new under the sun," our reaction to any present conflict is tempered by the realization that we have been this way before. While Protestant Christians accept the fact that there is no new truth, church history demonstrates to us that there is no new heresy either. The New Age movement offers nothing new to this age. We are dealing with "the same ol' stuff" in a different wrapper.

In presenting their meditation/visualization teachings to the church, Kelsey, Virkler, Wise, Foster, and others also appeal to the same historical precedent, but for the sake of defending their teaching. They accurately claim that the visualized encounter with the "real Jesus" (and Mary and sundry saints) had been a part of the experiences of the Catholic mystics of the past. Carl Jung himself undergirded his "spiritual" philosophy with the precedent of the ancient mystics and presented seminars on the *Spiritual Exercises* of Ignatius Loyola.[2]

Contemplative mysticism, the practice of meditating and looking within to find God, has never been accepted within historic Protestantism, and for good reason. William James points out: "Apart from what prayer may lead to, Protestant mystical experience appears to have been exclusively sporadic."[3] Catholic monastic Thomas Merton indicates that "the characteristic 'Protestant' reaction to mysticism has been a basic repugnance." According to Merton, Protestants have viewed mysticism as a denial of the Gospel or as a "gnosticism" which seeks to add to the Gospel certain elements of Greek contemplative philosophy. Merton accurately states that Protestants have emphasized religious experience, but it has been "prophetic" and not "contemplative."[4]

The Reformation emphasis upon Scripture alone, establishing the Gospel as the means for encountering the reality of the living Christ, leaves no room for a mysticism which seeks new truth and revelation in the introverted, contemplative spiritual encounter. For Reformation Protestantism to accept such mystical encounter and to acknowledge the objective reality of the visualized Jesus, the singular authority of Scripture and the gospel-based theology must first be set aside. From my perspective, one must discard his entire historical birthright to embrace the mystical encounter. The price is too high for what amounts to "old pottage."

Rather than embracing the ongoing revelation of contemplative mysticism, Reformation theology locates the supernatural Christian dynamic in the enlightening, illuminating work of the Holy Spirit upon the *existing external Word of God* so that we might prophetically "speak forth" the good news of God's grace revealed in Christ Jesus. We believe that the Holy Spirit comes to "lead us into all truth," not through mystical contemplation but by enlightening to our understanding the biblical record. Contrary to what some visualization advocates claim, rejecting contemplative mysticism does not leave dead, dogmatic rationalism as the only alternative. The biblical record of God's Word is alive, active, and highly productive.

Placing the inner-healing/visualization movement within the context of church history helps us to avoid some of the pitfalls of overreaction. For example, to promote a blanket condemnation of the entire field of psychology is, in my estimation, not operating historically but hysterically. Psychology has not created the problem but has merely redefined it. The "dog" is the same. Jungian psychology has simply built a new "doghouse."

Modern psychological research, especially that related to psychic phenomena, has been very helpful in understanding, if not debunking, the mystical experience. Such research, especially the insight gained by the "right-brained/left-brained" theory, provides a stronger argument for rejecting the "mystical encounter" than for accepting it. The meditative prelude necessary to engage the objects of imagination was thought of by the mystics of the past as being a divinely produced state of ecstasy or "orison." Today, modern psychology merely defines this ecstatic "spiritual" state as being the result of attaining alpha level and activating the right side of the brain, a condition able to be self-induced. *God has nothing to do with it!* The mystical experience, thanks to psychology, has been moved out of the dimension of the supernatural into the "natural." Once an alleged Christian experience becomes explainable in terms of "scientific" psychology, the mystery of the divine dynamic is removed and the experience loses credibility. It is similar to discovering the physiological or psychological basis for "love." Who needs it?

Understanding the historical context is also helpful in keeping us from placing too many eggs in our "end-of-the-world" basket. I am sure that deeper research into the past history of the church would expose the fact that intrusions of mysticism caused some Christians of the past to even declare, "This is the great deception to occur before the end of this age." If this deception becomes so widespread that introverted mysticism gains whole-sale acceptance within the church, and we conclude that it is indeed "the great falling away to take place before the end of this age," so be it. "Even so, come Lord Jesus." But somehow I have enough confidence in the preserving power of the Holy Spirit and the basic common sense of God's people to believe that there will be no wholesale acceptance of a psychological mysticism which reduces the sum and substance of Christian spiritual experience to unconscious brain waves.

Placing this deception within history also has a way of bursting the charismatic bubble of ecumenical idealism. It has always seemed to me that charismatics have lacked a sensitivity to the history of the development of theology, often viewing doctrinal differences defining denominational boundaries as "works of the flesh" rather than as efforts on the part of sincere Christians of the past to preserve truth. The visualization/inner-healing debate brings us back to the reality that the dynamic experience of Catholics and Protestants "singing in tongues" together does not change the fact that the two camps promote a different under-standing of the authority of Scripture. Such an important difference cannot be eliminated by a euphoric experience.

BACK TO SCRIPTURE

We began with the question of the authority of Scripture and then traced inner healing and visualization through the maze of psychological theory. Even apart from any consideration of the lack of biblical foundation, the psychological principles upon which inner healing and visualization are based certainly provide sufficient reason to reject the teaching. Yet, after all the psycho-logical theories are unmasked and the faulty logic and reasoning of the inner-healing teachers revealed, it is only proper that we end where we began: with the question of the authority of Scrip-ture. We must underline the fact that this remains *the prime issue*.

In the very beginning I stated that I believed that the charis-matic movement brings a significant contribution to the life of the church. I believe this with all my heart. The movement has much to offer in terms of spiritual life and vitality. The tragedy is that we charismatics have had a tendency to self-destruct, dulling our witness with our extrabiblical theological silliness and outlandish prophetic claims.

Why does it seem so difficult for charismatic teachers to stay within the boundaries of Scripture in offering their message to the church? Is it so distasteful to teach what the Bible clearly teaches rather than pursuing new revelations and new truths? Is it somehow "unspiritual" for a charismatic to desire sound methods of biblical interpretation that result in good theology?

It is tragic to see charismatics being blown to and fro by questionable and deceptive teachings while at the same time lacking a basic understanding of some of the rudimentary truths of New Testament Christianity. They run to inner-healing seminars, get "slain in the Spirit" one more time, attend "centering prayer workshops," have their family trees healed, have their dreams interpreted, name and claim their blessings, place their faith in their faith, seek to create their desires by visualization, and stand on tiptoes waiting for a new wave of the Spirit—yet many of them do not have the slightest understanding of what the Bible teaches about our righteousness before God and what it means to live and walk in Christ Jesus. It is a tragedy.

Self-Rejection

13

Self-Rejection

Every Christian wrestles with the question of sanctification, with the conflicts of the "flesh desiring against the spirit, and the spirit against the flesh" (Galatians 5:17). The ministry of inner healing claims to offer relief from nagging sins and compulsive behavior, leading to the hope of sanctification. The ministry is based upon the Freudian premise that the traumas and hurts of the past become buried within the unconscious mind and influence, if not actually determine, human behavior. The methodology of inner healing employs the Jungian concept of active imagination to reach the unconscious hurts and apply the healing love of Jesus.

The true biblical understanding of the Christian life and sanctification also possesses both *premise* and *methodology*. In this chapter we will consider the biblical understanding of the Christian life, the premise upon which it is built. We will follow with a discussion of the methodology employed in our day-to-day living.

THE QUEST

After entering the ministry in 1965 I soon saw that, while I may have been prepared theologically, I was not adequately prepared spiritually. It was a rude awakening after spending years in an academic surrounding and possessing minimal interest in practical spirituality. This is not a criticism of my college or seminary training; spiritual life was there if I wanted it. But I was not adequately interested—personal spirituality was not one of my top priorities.

Being thrust into a parish situation has a way of producing many insecurities, especially if you know you are not what your people think you are. Stirring up determination or making resolutions regarding your spiritual life never work. Such efforts simply include you in the outworking of Romans chapter 7: You don't do the good you want to do, but instead you do the evil you wish to avoid. Being unwilling to accept the "ministerial charade" and be satisfied with the double life, I decided to do something about it, to pursue a course of study which would provide answers.

I threw myself into a pursuit of Christian ethics. Beginning with the Greek philosophers, I studied the questions of good and evil, right and wrong as they applied to personal living. This was the age of the "new morality" and "situation ethics." I was not so much interested in discovering a system of ethics that would *adjust* my life, but rather in discovering a system that would *match* my life. I was not prepared to drop "the standard" and accept new morality, but somehow I felt that the standard had to be interpreted in such a way as to at least provide some reachable goal. I believed in the forgiveness available in Christ Jesus but was not willing to settle for the "sin-and-get-forgiven" scenario as standard operating procedure. The New Testament certainly demanded more in terms of growth in Christ Jesus. I concluded my study with the complex ethical reasonings of Dietrich Bonhoeffer. While Bonhoeffer moaned the existence of cheap grace, his ethical system did not provide a way of turning cheap grace into costly discipleship. I arrived at the conclusion that the answer was not to be found in ethical systems based upon varying degrees of willpower, determination, and self-discipline, since I was not blessed with any of those qualities.

After my brief escapade into the realm of psychological encounter turned from a potential help into actual heresy, I became involved in the charismatic movement. I experienced the reality and power of the Holy Spirit, and for the first time in my life I had an experience with God that produced life-changing results. The presence of Jesus in my life was very real. Prayer and the study of Scripture were no longer a chore but a joy, not a discipline or duty but a daily dynamic. While many elements in my life were adjusted, many of the old habits, temptations, weaknesses, and personality wrinkles remained.

TRY AGAIN

The old "quest for holiness" was stirred again, but this time in a different direction. After reading and rereading the Watchman Nee classic *The Normal Christian Life* I was convinced that the answer to the Romans 7 dilemma—that man was unable to do the good he wanted to do and avoid the evil he hated—was to be found in Romans 8. This was not a very profound discovery, since the truth presented by the apostle Paul in Romans is consecutive in nature. The only problem was that I did not understand what Paul was talking about in Romans 8.

Two statements made by Paul in that chapter caused me all kinds of problems:

> The law of the Spirit of life in Christ Jesus has set me free from the law of sin and death.
> The just requirement of the law [is] fulfilled in [us] who walk not according to the flesh but according to the Spirit (Romans 8:2,4).

I knew what "the law of sin and death" involved. Paul used the phrase to describe the seemingly hopeless Romans 7 experience. But what was "the law of the Spirit of life in Christ Jesus" which sets one free from "the law of sin and death"? How did that law operate? I desired the "righteousness of the law" in my daily experience, but what did it mean that such righteousness was experienced by "walking according to the Spirit"? How was this to be accomplished? Through prayer and study I was intently involved in this quest for at least six months.

Finally one November afternoon the light began to dawn. I was standing by our back patio door looking out at the trees in the woods behind the house. The trees are a variety of oak which retain their old brown leaves throughout the winter. It seemed as if the Holy Spirit put the question in my mind, "How do those trees lose their old leaves?"

"Well," I thought, "in the spring when the sap moves up from the roots into the trunk and into the branches and twigs, the old leaves fall off and new buds come forth in their place."

"Those trees are just like you," the Holy Spirit continued to teach, "but unlike those trees, you try to shake off the old leaves rather than to trust the new life that is within you. You keep looking at yourself rather than looking at Jesus. Stir up the new life that you have in Christ Jesus, for in that life is the power to set you free from sin and death."

I pondered the thoughts. The words of Jesus in John 15:5 came to mind: "I am the vine, you are the branches. He who abides in me and I in him, he it is that bears much fruit, for apart from me you can do nothing." The key to the Christian life, according to our Lord Jesus, was *to abide in Him or to walk after the Spirit*.

I began to see that God had given me only one thing—His Son, Jesus—but that in Christ Jesus were to be found all things pertaining to life and salvation. I was saved by His life! He does not *remake* me so that I am obedient, or holy, or righteous, but He *is* all of these things to me. He is my wisdom, my righteousness, my sanctification, my redemption (1 Corinthians 1:30). For me it was a new revelation based on the enlightenment of God's Word to see that the Christian life was not a set of moral prescriptions which will sanctify in the doing of them. Instead, the Christian life is *the life of Christ at work in me*. Only one Person had ever truly lived that life, and He desired, by the working of the Holy Spirit, to live it in me. As God had only given me one thing, so He also expected of me only one thing—to abide in Christ Jesus. By abiding in Him, the righteousness of the law would be fulfilled in me. I would be set free from the law of sin and death. I had finally discovered the ethical simplicity that is in Christ Jesus.

NOT I, BUT . . .

I soon discovered that the outworking of these truths involved a drastic adjustment in how I viewed myself. Before I could experience the new life in Christ, I had to regard myself as dead, "lifeless." In order to "find my life" in Christ, I had to first "lose my life."

There are many verses in the New Testament which define and describe the working of the life of Christ Jesus within. Yet the prerequisite for living that life involves death. In Galatians 2:20 the apostle Paul writes:

> I have been crucified with Christ; it is no longer I who live, but Christ who lives in me; and the life I now live in the flesh I live by faith in the Son of God, who loved me and gave himself for me.

Paul says that, even though he has been crucified with Christ, he still lives, but the life that he lives is Christ dwelling within him. The King James Version of the Bible puts it this way: "Nevertheless I live, YET NOT I, but Christ liveth in me." Paul views himself as being dead to himself.

In Romans 6 the apostle declares that we are dead as far as sin is concerned. We are to think of ourselves as dead to sin and alive to God (Romans 6:11). In Romans 7:1-12 he tells us that we are dead as far as the law and righteousness is concerned. Obviously if we are *dead* we can no longer commit sins, nor can we perform any good deeds of righteousness. We are dead! The apostle clearly expresses this reality in Colossians 3:1-3:

> If then you have been raised with Christ, seek the things that are above, where Christ is, seated at the right hand of God. Set your minds on things that are above, not on things that are on earth. FOR YOU HAVE DIED, and your life is hid with Christ in God. When CHRIST WHO IS OUR LIFE appears, then you also will appear with him in glory.

Very few Christians realize that the key to the Christian life and experience is not self-acceptance or self-esteem or developing a positive self-image. The key is *self-rejection*. Thinking of yourself as dead is the ultimate act of rejection. When Jesus said, "If any man will come after me, he must deny himself, take up his cross, and follow me," He was not referring to giving up ice cream for Lent. Self-denial is not denying certain pleasures to self but is *denying self*, rejecting self. By taking up your cross and following Jesus, you are going to die! It is that simple. We make a terrible mistake in thinking that Jesus wants to give us a positive self-image, that the Christian faith is geared to enlarging us, increasing our self-esteem, putting our lives together. The very opposite is true: "We must decrease while He must increase." In our weakness, the strength of Christ is manifested and brought into maturity.

If you read the epistles of Paul with a view to his own personal experience, you note a unique combination of self-abasement and Christ-esteem. While possessing a deep awareness of his own miserable condition as being "the chief of sinners," he also possessed an equally deep awareness of the greatness of the life of Christ Jesus at work in him. The two go hand in hand. The more we come to know the Lord, the less we think of ourselves. The less confidence we have in ourselves, the more we need Jesus. If we arrive at the conclusion that there is absolutely no hope of sanctification and holiness in us, that *we are dead*, we will desire to find all of our righteousness in Christ Jesus, *who becomes our life*.

Think of yourself in this way: You have died. You are laid out in a casket. Jesus comes to you and takes your hand. His life begins to flow through you. You arise and, holding on to the hand of Jesus, you walk with Him. His life flows through your will, your emotions, your mind, your natural talents, your abilities. *You live*, but it is not your life: *Christ is living in you and through you*. If one day you decide to drop His hand and go your own way, you crumple into a heap because actually you are dead! It is *Christ* who is your life! According to the teachings of the New Testament we are to think of ourselves in this way, and it involves the ultimate self-rejection. It is not the rejection of our personhood— our will, our feelings, our mind, our natural talents and abilities—but is the rejection of the life we received from Adam which animates these natural functions of our person.

The ministry of inner healing, because it is based upon principles drawn from the field of psychology, is directed at self-acceptance rather than self-rejection. Inner healing attempts to improve the human condition. But according to Scripture God is not involved in "repair work." Instead, He replaces our broken lives with the life of Christ. In fact, it is in our brokenness and in our weakness that the life of Christ is most clearly manifested in us. Jesus does not promise to go back in our memories, dig up past events, and repair us. He *does* promise and offer to us His life as a substitute, encouraging us to abide in Him. By receiving that life we continue to live, but it is no longer we who live but Christ who lives in us.

The problem is that we do not want to be replaced, even if it is with the life of Jesus. We do not want to die and come to an end of ourselves. We prefer to get better, because we think that there is something good in us that is worth preserving. We do not want to direct our conscious thinking away from ourselves and toward Jesus. We would much prefer to sit quietly, examine our own psyche, and rehearse all the incidents of the past in which we were victimized, feeling sorry for ourselves in the process.

THE FIRST INTENTION

Many Christian do not realize that God's purpose is not to make them personally righteous but to manifest the righteousness of Christ within them. Jesus is our wisdom, our righteousness, our sanctification, our redemption (1 Corinthians 1:30). Not being clear on this divine purpose, they accept the mistaken notion that God is out to make them supersanctified Christians in and of themselves. People will look at them, so they think, and declare, "There goes a great man (or woman) of God," How glorious it will be!

After they come into relationship with Jesus Christ and are filled with the Holy Spirit, God's initial intention is not to strengthen them or to mightily use them, but to weaken them, bringing them to an end of themselves.

This divine intention is often initiated through what I have been calling the Romans 7 dilemma. Many Christians never get out of this dilemma because they never understand the purpose for it. The dilemma works something like this: We become Christians filled with the Holy Spirit who set out to do great things for God, to live for God, to be holy for God. Looking at our lives, we discover that there are many problems that must be overcome if we are to be good Christians. We decide that we are going to "shape up for Jesus." God, so we think, is going to help us in this task. He will make us strong, giving us greater willpower and determination.

After we set out on this noble endeavor we eventually arrive at the conclusion, much to our dismay, that we are not experiencing much progress. The "old leaves" do not readily fall off the tree. We become stuck in the middle of Romans 7: The good we *want* to do we *don't* do, and the evil we want to *stop* doing we do anyway. So we cry out to God, "O Lord, help me. Strengthen me. Enable me to do Your will." We get up, clean ourselves off, and determine with new resolve to try harder. But it still doesn't work.

Finally we arrive at the conclusion that we are missing some necessary ingredient in order to accomplish our task. There has to be some type of ministry we can receive which will solve the dilemma. We decide to make the rounds through various charismatic ministries. We get the demons cast out. We get "slain in the Spirit" one more time. We try inner healing. We seek to get our family tree healed, or the curse removed from our bloodline. Yet we find no lasting relief.

"WRETCHED MAN THAT I AM"

Instead of running around trying to solve the Romans 7 dilemma by false solutions, if we would take the time to read to the end of Romans 7 and search out the biblical understanding of the Christian life we would discover where God has been trying to lead us all along. Note the response of the apostle Paul: As a result of his own Romans 7 dilemma he declared, "Wretched man that I am!" He came to an end of himself. He looked at his condition and declared, "I am a wretch!"

Many Christians never come to the point of declaring, "Wretched man that I am!" They keep thinking that somewhere, somehow there has to be help so they can do the things they want to do and stop doing the things they don't want to do. But that is not God's purpose. This "wretched man" declaration in Romans 7:24 is the door into the new life depicted in Romans 8: "There is therefore now no condemnation for those who are in Christ Jesus. For the law of the Spirit of life in Christ Jesus has set me free from the law of sin and death" (Romans 8:1,2).

Arriving at the end of Romans 7 by personal experience is not all that easy. It is very difficult to come to the point of self-rejection, to see ourselves as being wretched. By doing this we are acknowledging that there is something wrong with us. While we may accept the theological position that we are born in sin and that there is nothing good within our human nature, and while we may even quote the Bible verse stating that "all our righteousness is as filthy rags," it is very, very difficult to personally apply these truths to our lives and arrive at the conclusion that *we are the problem.*

It is far easier to view our problems as the result of injustices inflicted upon us by other people. "We are not wretched," we reason. "We were simply the victims of some wretched experiences, or are possessed by wretched demons, or had a wretched family tree." Because our lives are born in Adam, we have inherited the Adam-and-Eve-syndrome. After falling into sin Adam declared, "Lord, it wasn't my fault. It was that woman You gave me." Confronted with Adam's accusation, Eve declared, "Lord, it wasn't my fault, it was that miserable snake."

Note how this works out in practice. People run from job to job, from marriage to marriage, and from church to church but never discover contentment, peace, or joy. They are always blaming something or someone else for their problems. Isn't it amazing that they never come to the point of stopping, taking a good close look at themselves, and realistically asking, "Could it be that I am the problem?"

It is contrary to the will and purpose of God to stop, adjust, change, or heal the process depicted in Romans chapter 7. It is the desire of God to continually bring us to an end of ourselves and to new beginnings in Christ Jesus. The process never stops. Sometimes we think we are dead when in fact we have only fainted. Our old life is continually trying to stick up its ugly head. Apart from human weakness there is no repentance, no turning to Jesus, no receiving Him anew as our life. If all the hurts of the past which produce negative behavior and bring us to the "O wretched man that I am" conclusion were healed by God, He would be going contrary to His own purpose of replacing "self" with the life of Christ. God continually has to deal with us—to discipline us and prune us so that we depend upon the life of Christ Jesus and not upon our own human strength, willpower, and determination.

Abiding in Christ

14

Abiding in Christ

It is one thing to talk about *what* God wants us to do but something else again to understand *how* He wants us to do it. Within the context of Christianity we are more geared to talking about the *what* of God than the *how* of God. If the key to the Christian life is abiding in Christ, the question of *how* we are supposed to abide in Christ is very important.

In this area of method we need to move very carefully. Considering the nature of the present deception, I am sure that someone is going to suggest that counting oneself down to alpha level, visualizing Jesus, and then fellowshiping with "Him" is *abiding in Christ*. Such mystical action is probably the ultimate act of "abiding in yourself." By claiming that we are able to alter human consciousness in order to find Jesus is certainly not an act of self-rejection.

Let us be certain that our methods are biblical methods.

LEARNING TO ABIDE

In Romans 8:5-7, immediately following the verses in which we are told that the righteousness of the law is fulfilled in those who walk in the Spirit, the apostle Paul sets down some very specific directions:

> Those who live according to the flesh set their minds
> on the things of the flesh, but those who live according
> to the Spirit set their minds on the things of the Spirit.
> To set the mind on the flesh is death, but to set the mind
> on the Spirit is life and peace.

According to these very clear verses, the mind established on the things of the Spirit will produce life and peace, but the mind

established on the things of the flesh will result in death (separa-
tion from the life that is in Christ Jesus). If I am to abide in Christ
and experience freedom from the law of sin and death, I must
learn to establish my mind upon the things of the Spirit.

In the light of the present-day deception it is necessary to point
out that the Greek word for "mind" in Romans 8:5,6 is *phro-
nema*, which means "intentions, affections, and desires." It is the
same word used in Colossians 3:2, in which the apostle tells us to
"set our affections above, where Christ is seated at the right hand
of God." The word has absolutely nothing to do with forming
mental images of Jesus.

After every Sunday sermon, as a traditional practice followed
by many pastors in our church, I would conclude by saying, "And
the peace of God, which passes all understanding, will keep your
hearts and your minds in Christ Jesus." One Sunday it hit me.
What I am saying is *what I want*! I want to have my heart and my
mind kept in Christ Jesus, because "in Christ Jesus" are all things
pertaining to life, to joy, to hope, to salvation.

I went to the fourth chapter of Philippians and read that verse in
the context. The apostle was instructing these Christians how to
live in Christ, to walk in the Spirit. He began in verse 4 by telling
them to rejoice in the Lord always. He continued by instructing
them not to get all upset about the situations of life, because the
Lord was coming soon. "Don't worry," he said, "Let God know
your concerns and bring them to Him with thanksgiving." As a
result, "the peace of God that passes all understanding will keep
your hearts and minds in Christ." In conclusion, he told them to
set their minds upon good things.

MEETING THE ENEMY

In attempting to put into practice the biblical directive to set
my mind upon the things of the Spirit, I noticed something very
interesting about the direction of my thoughts, desires, and affections. While I had come to the conclusion that all my problems

began with me and that I was my own worst enemy, I did not realize how profoundly this fact worked out in practice. I took note of how much of my day-to-day thinking involved *me*. I was the center of my own conscious attention. In order to live and walk in Christ Jesus, I had to make a *conscious rejection of me*. While it is one thing to reject yourself in theory, it is something quite different to do it in practice. Self-rejection implies *not giving self a place* in my conscious thought life. This is not easy to do, because I don't want to do it. I want to center my thoughts and my attention upon *me*. If somebody hurts me or if something terrible happens to me, I have a right to feel sorry for myself, so I thought. If I am attacked, I have a right to defend myself. I have a right to worry about myself. After all, if I don't, who will? Detaching yourself from yourself in practice means bringing every thought captive to the obedience of Christ (2 Corinthians 10:5).

Actually, I came to see that all the works of the flesh proceed from a self-centered existence. Jesus' Sermon on the Mount—His teaching on turning the other cheek, going the extra mile, and rejoicing in persecution—defined and described a life in which self had no place. Jesus did not teach these things in order to create a kingdom of people who lived in resignation to the way things were, becoming the doormats of other people. Jesus' teachings were directed at showing us how to live in joy and peace in the midst of the circumstances of life, whether past, present, or future. When Paul and Silas were singing praises in the prison at Philippi they were not showing off their piety or their profound spirituality. They had learned how to be happy and content in the midst of all situations. If Jesus was to be my life, *I had to go*, not only in theory but in practice.

The book of Genesis describes the events of creation and the fall into sin. In those first chapters we see that the devil's purpose was not to create a conflict between himself and God, but rather to drive a wedge *between man and God*. In the fall, man chose to live by the knowledge of good and evil rather than by his day-to-day relationship with God.

In my estimation, the major work of the devil is to turn people in on themselves, to center their conscious attention upon themselves, their circumstances, their plight in life, their worries, their fears, their failures, their successes, the events in the past in which they were victimized. The purpose of the Holy Spirit is to turn us away from ourselves unto Jesus, so that in Him we might live and walk. The Bible directs us to set our attention—our conscious, moment-by-moment focus—above, where Christ is seated at the right hand of God.

I began to teach the truths that I was learning to my congregation, with great results. I could see that the possibility existed that we could live in joy and peace by simply becoming conscious of the direction of our lives, the thoughts and intentions of our hearts and minds. I taught people, after first applying it to myself, how to "kick out" the unwelcome intruders that enter our minds, especially the thoughts that are centered in or directed at ourselves. This was, in fact, "repentance," the conscious changing of the mind and setting the thoughts on the things of Jesus. I learned the vitally important principle that all teaching relating to the Christian life and experience must exist at the point *where the branch meets the Vine*.

TRAGEDY

One day I got the tragic news that a man in our congregation had died suddenly of a heart attack. Even though his wife, Mary, was one of the spiritually renewed members of our congregation, I knew it was going to be a very difficult situation. Mary was alone, since they had no children. I also knew that Mary possessed an uncanny fear of funeral homes. She had attended one funeral in her life, from which she was carried out screaming and crying.

I arrived at their home and found Mary in an emotionally distraught condition, which was obviously to be expected. A number of members of our congregation were already at the home, attempting to apply some comfort, some assurrance, some hope. We prayed together and shared the Word together, but the combination of grief, fear, and uncertainty produced a tremendous obstacle against the application of divine promise. It was not a question of heaven or hell; both Mary and her husband believed in Jesus, and she knew that there would be a reunion in heaven. The problem was getting through the present situation. I knew that the next day, with the initial visit to the funeral home and the open casket, would be highly traumatic. Some of Mary's friends stayed with her through that night.

I returned to the home the next morning and discovered a totally different situation. While Mary was filled with grief and sorrow over the loss of her husband, whom she deeply loved, her eyes were also aglow with joy and peace. Something had happened. After giving her a big hug, I looked at her eye-to-eye and asked, "What happened to you?"

"Last night," she began to explain, "I was crying out to God. 'Why Lord? Why me? What am I going to do? How will I make it through the days ahead?' In the midst of my crying out to God a little voice within me said, 'Mary, if you will praise me I will give you my peace.' I stopped praying. I stopped asking. While it was so difficult, I lifted my hands in the air and began to worship the Lord. I confessed my dependency upon Him, knowing that all things in my life will work for good. As I praised," Mary explained, "the peace of God filled my life."

I will never forget seeing Mary standing next to the open casket that night at the funeral home. Her husband was well known and loved in the community, so the funeral home was very crowded. While her eyes were filled with tears and they were rolling freely down her cheeks, a genuine glow of joy and peace emanated from her. Mary never repressed her grief; it was freely expresed. Yet in the midst of the grief her heart and her mind were kept securely in Christ Jesus. She was experiencing His life in her. Today, over ten years later, that joy and peace remains.

AN IMPORTANT LESSON

I learned a very important lesson from that situation. In my dealings with people, in my counseling, I always made room for legitimate self-pity, legitimate fear and worry, legitimate depression. I functioned toward people with the understanding that the experience of a real tragedy allowed for a measure of self-indulgence. The traumatic experiences of the past, I thought, should realistically produce negative response. I permitted people to respond to past traumatic situations as I would respond, since we are all only human. I could have never said to Mary the same day her husband died, "Stop feeling sorry for yourself and praise Jesus!" From my perspective it would have been cruel. Yet that is exactly what the Holy Spirit told her. From what I have learned, God simply does not allow us the privilege of emotional self-indulgence.

This is not to suggest that compassion and empathy have no place within the body of Christ; the Bible tells us to be "kind and tenderhearted" and "to bear one another's burdens." Yet we are also instructed to "speak the truth in love," including the truth that we should "give thanks in all situations of life" and "rejoice in the Lord always." The real question that we need to think through is, How does the love of Jesus function in our relationships with other people?

Every negative element in our lives in which we fall short of the glory of God and entertain the flesh begins with a thought, a desire, an affection. For this reason the apostle Paul speaks of bringing every thought captive to the obedience of Christ, renewing our minds, and setting our hearts and minds upon Jesus. This is not a passive practice in which we sit quietly in a chair, empty our minds, and visualize Jesus. It is an active, day-by-day, moment-by-moment conscious appropriation of the life we have in Christ.

We do not have to entertain thoughts of lust, fear, worry, and self-pity. We can choose to expel them, worship Jesus, and abide in Him. I realize that there are people who over the years have confirmed themselves in a specific style of compulsive behavior. There are people who are compulsive worriers, confirmed in that attitude. It has become their lifestyle. Rebuilding their will, their decision regarding worry, becomes a process. They need to repent, to change their mind, to put out the thought, to nip worry in the bud 40 times a day. The good news is that the next day it may be only 35 times!

THE NEW REFORMATION

When I first entered the ministry I would at times spend days, if not weeks, indulged in self-pity. Actually, I met with a group of other pastors on a regular basis for what we thought was a time of encouraging each other, building up each other, and bearing and sharing each other's burdens as "we suffered through the heat of the day, serving the Lord." As I look back, I was really a member of the 4P club: the poor pastor's pity party. It was a sick situation! I have come to the conclusion that if a man is in the full-time Christian ministry and wallows in self-pity, thinking of his vocation in terms of "suffering through the heat of the day," he ought to find a new line of work.

There are still times when I indulge myself in self-pity, but there is one major difference: Now I know how to get out of it. It may only last for a few moments. I have discovered that the difference between maturity and immaturity in Christ is not found in whether a person indulges from time to time in the perverted thinking of the flesh, since temptations will come. Maturity in Christ is knowing how to get up and get out of the situation and to find the way of escape.

The attitude that we maintain toward self is a key in the whole subject of abiding in Christ Jesus. I have learned not to take myself too seriously, but to take my relationship with the Lord Jesus very seriously. I have clearly taught this way of thinking within my congregations. It makes a profound difference in the manner in which Christians relate to each other.

If in a gathering one member begins to complain about his or her plight in life, it is not unusual for the group to look at the complaining member and sadly declare, "Ah, poor you." It is vitally important within the fellowship of the body of Christ that we remind each other to turn away from self and turn to Jesus and abide in Him. Those who join Christian groups to participate in the game of "Can you top this?" in problem-sharing would not discover much ego-soothing within some of our fellowships.

Such interaction within the body of Christ never ignores the reality of legitimate pain, grief, or sorrow, nor forgets that Christ dwelling in us manifests Himself in love and compassion. But the purpose of that love and compassion is to bring help, encouragement, and even admonition so that the hurting member of the body is reminded to stay joined to the *Head* even in the midst of pain and sorrow. There are times when such admonition is brought with a note of humor, while at other times it is offered in a sorrowful embrace. Yet the same intention remains: *Abide in Christ!*

Having a low estimate of yourself and a high estimate of Jesus produces incredible freedom. You are finally free from defending, preserving, and promoting self. Any of the events in your life which have produced in you a low self-esteem are blessings in disguise. You can laugh at yourself and raise your hands in worship of the Lord Jesus Christ, who has become your life. The more you esteem Jesus, the less you will esteem yourself. The more you worship the Lord Jesus, the less you will seek to preserve and defend yourself. If you knew Jesus in all His glory and majesty, you would despise yourself. Job declared, "I had heard of thee by the hearing of the ear, but now my eyes see thee; therefore I despise myself, and repent in dust and ashes" (Job 42:5,6).

Robert Schuller promotes the notion that self-esteem will produce a new reformation in the church of Jesus Christ. In my estimation nothing could be further from the truth. The church of

Jesus Christ will experience profound reformation, revival, restoration, and renewal as God's people with one accord worship, praise, and lift up the name of our Lord Jesus Christ, exalting Him as King of Kings and Lord of Lords. May we turn away from ourselves and worship Jesus!!

Not I But Christ

15

Not I But Christ

It is not easy to give up on yourself and declare, "There is no hope." Our human pride is always driving us to believe that we can get better, that there is something valuable within our human nature which is worth saving. In spite of the misery that is often associated with our lives, we want to keep hanging on to ourselves, not realizing that we are sick unto death, beyond healing. The devil's most important task is to turn us to ourselves.

For about the first six or seven years of my stay in Michigan I was involved off and on in counseling with a young woman named Ann. As a young girl she had been sexually abused by her father. As a result she was never able to find happiness in marriage. She equated love with sex.

After three divorces she met Hank, "Fell in love," and got married. In fact, I married them. The marriage worked out very well, because Hank loved Ann and was a strong authority figure. Psychologically, he was the loving "father-image" which Ann never had. One day as Hank was crawling out from under his automobile where he had been working, his foot kicked the jack and the car fell on him, killing him instantly.

Just a few months after the funeral, Ann began carousing through the bars again, seeking "love." Hank's family became very critical of her, describing her character in no uncertain terms. Ann became extremely upset and came to share her problems with me.

After tearfully describing her circumstances she said, "Oh, Pastor, I can't get any lower. I have never been so miserable."

"You know, Ann," I began to explain, "there is help. You can give up on yourself and accept Jesus. . . ."

I began to share with her the new life we can live in Christ Jesus. It was something I had wanted to do for a long time, but I had never sensed that she was ready or willing to listen. She was not coming to me for answers, but only for assurance. Because of her background, I did not want to reject her or turn her off. She continued to come to church from time to time. The door was open. Finally, I thought, she would be ready to listen, since she had hit bottom. As I continued to describe the great benefit of living in relationship with the Lord Jesus, an amazing thing began to happen. She stopped crying and wiped her eyes. Her face began to harden. She took out a cigarette and lit it. Then she interrupted me.

"I am not ready for that yet!" she said with cold determination. She began to get up and head for the door. I grabbed her arm.

"Ann, there is help available. When you are ready, will you come back and talk?"

She said that she would and then left. I never saw her again.

In over 20 years in the ministry I had never met anyone whose life was as messed up as Ann's, yet she responded, "I am not ready for that yet." It is not easy to turn away from yourself, even when you think you have hit bottom. Those who hit bottom are often more willing to turn to drugs or to alcohol than to turn to Jesus. But those who do reject themselves and accept Jesus as their life discover great results. It is only in being willing to lose ourselves that we find our real life in Christ Jesus.

"I CAN'T DO ANYTHING RIGHT"

A number of years ago a young woman by the name of Susan who lived in a neighboring community made an appointment to see me. Sitting down in my office, together with my secretary, she poured out a sad story of fear, frustration, and failure. From her perspective, her father had never affirmed her. While her brothers were continually built up in his eyes, she was always told, "You never do anything right. You will never amount to anything." She was an excellent candidate for inner healing. The diagnosis would be, "The inner child was still smarting from the father's rejection and needs to be embraced in the love of Jesus."

Susan's fear of failure hindered her from ever "doing anything right." Just the week before, her husband had planned on bringing home someone from work for supper. When it came time that day for Susan to begin to prepare supper, she froze, unable to even begin the task for fear of failure. Her husband arrived home and much to his dismay found that supper was not prepared and that his wife had spent a good part of the day in bed.

A friend in the prayer group of which she was a part told her that she probably had a demon of fear or a spirit of rejection. Since we were the "charismatic church" in the area, she figured that we were "doing deliverance." She came up to see me for the express purpose of having the demon of fear or rejection cast out.

For years Susan had been involved in psychotherapy. For six months she had been an outpatient at a local mental hospital. Susan was a young woman in her thirties, quite attractive but very confused. She was a committed Christian and had experienced the reality of the Holy Spirit in her life. For a brief time the experience of the Holy Spirit had produced a positive effect, but then she fell back into the old patterns of fear and failure.

After pouring out the sad story of her difficult childhood she began to cry.

"Sometimes I feel like I can't do anything right," she sobbed. "I feel like I am completely worthless."

After a few moments of silence I responded very slowly and softly, "Maybe you *are* completely worthless."

She was startled. She looked up with anger in her eyes and said, "No one ever told me that before! My psychiatrist always tells me that I am a valuable person, that I should develop a good self-image, that I . . ."

"Has it worked?" I interrupted.

"Well, no," she admitted, "but I am not ready to give up on myself. I am a valuable human being."

"What if," I suggested, "giving up on yourself is the key to new life, the key to help? Would you be willing to reject yourself if you were able to accept the Lord Jesus as your substitute?"

I opened my Bible and began to share with her the dilemma of Paul in Romans 7. She related very much to Paul's conflict. I pointed out to her that her statement of feeling completely worthless corresponds to Paul declaring, "O wretched man that I am." We proceeded into Romans 8. I explained to her that the apostle Paul discovered the answer to his dilemma in Christ Jesus. The "law of the spirit of life in Christ Jesus" had set him free from the "law of sin and death." We looked at the third chapter of Colossians, in which the apostle speaks of himself as being dead and that Christ is his life. We reviewed the truth of Galatians 2:20, that Christ is to live out His life in us.

"While you may be a failure, Susan, Jesus has never failed at anything He set out to do!" I explained to her. "If you learn to abide in Him by establishing your heart and mind in Him, He will do in you what you are not able to do."

I taught Susan how to get off herself and live in Christ Jesus by rejecting any thoughts that are self-centered. I taught her how to repent of self-directed thinking and to respond to the Lord with praise and worship. We talked about the verses in Romans 8 in which the apostle tells us that the "mind set on the Spirit produces life and peace."

I explained to Susan very clearly that she had one problem, and it was Susan. She had to reject herself, get out of the way, kick out all self-centered thinking, and allow the "law of the Spirit of life in Christ Jesus" to work. We prayed together. Susan confessed to the Lord that she was a failure and had come to the end of seeking to make herself successful. She asked the Lord Jesus to live out His life in her.

I never saw Susan again, but I did receive some good news about her progress. Two years later, at an area pastors' conference, the pastor in one of the churches in the community where Susan lived asked me if I remembered her. I said that I did. He continued:

"Last week she was the speaker at our large ladies' gathering. She told us about your advice to her. She

spoke on the theme 'I can do all things through Christ
who strengthens me.' "

I almost fell off my chair. This woman who was unable to
prepare supper for her husband was now a public speaker, sharing
the good news of rejecting yourself and accepting Jesus as your
life!

What I told Susan was the direct opposite of what she had been
receiving in counseling. While her psychiatrist was attempting to
build a positive self-image, developing self-esteem, I taught her to
accept the negative self-image. While psychotherapy was leading
her to self-acceptance, I led her into self-rejection and "Christ-
acceptance."

I QUIT!

A number of years ago I conducted a weeklong series of
teachings in a basement prayer meeting in Grand Rapids, Michigan. One evening, as the meeting came to a close, I went over to
the punch bowl in the corner of the basement to be alone for a few
minutes.

My brief moment of privacy was invaded by an angry-looking
man stomping over to the punch bowl to have a drink.

"Good evening, how are you doing?" I greeted him.

"Aw," he answered, "I can't stand these meetings. My wife
always drags me away from the TV in hopes that I will become
spiritual."

I began to laugh. We introduced ourselves. His name was
Steve. "Why don't you enjoy these gatherings?" I asked. "These
are some real nice people."

"It's all that lovey-dovey, praise-the-Lord, hallelujah stuff that
I can't handle. I'm just not that kind of person."

As we continued the conversation, he shared with me that he
was born and raised in a home where emotions, especially love,
were never outwardly demonstrated.

"I'm really not able to love people," he admitted. "There are
people I work with that I genuinely can't stand. In fact, I guess
there are people I hate. I'm not ashamed to say it. It's a fact."

"Are you happy with that kind of attitude?" I asked.

"Not really, but what can I do? That's how I'm made up." He shrugged his shoulders in simple resignation to the way things were. "Oh, I try to be nice to other people, but it doesn't work."

"So what you are telling me," I summarized, "is that you are by nature an unloving, hateful, angry, antisocial person."

"Well, maybe I'm not that bad," he objected. "But . . ."

"Wait a minute, Steve," I interrupted, "tell it the way it is. Have you not resigned yourself to maintaining an unloving attitude toward other people?"

"I guess so," he admitted. "But what can I do? That's the way I am."

"Do you think that's the way Jesus is?" I asked.

"Of course not. Jesus loves other people," he quickly answered.

"Do you believe in Jesus?"

"Sure I do," he answered. "I'm a Christian."

"If you believe in Jesus, He lives in you by His Holy Spirit. Doesn't this also mean that Jesus is able to love people through you? In other words, don't you think Jesus' love for other people can come through you?"

Steve thought for a moment and then replied, "I guess so."

"Are you willing to let Him do it?" I asked.

"What must I do? Remember, I'm not interested in becoming like these lovey-dovey, praise-the-Lord people," he answered quite firmly.

I explained to him that Jesus would not violate his will.

"The key in all this," I continued, "is that you must get out of the way. In other words, you must admit to the Lord Jesus that you are an unloving, hateful person and invite Him to love others through you. Are you willing?"

"All right, I'll give it a try."

I led him in a prayer. He confessed his miserable, unloving nature and told the Lord Jesus that he would quit trying to love other people. He invited Jesus to do it in him.

I explained to Steve that the next morning he should reaffirm his desire to let Jesus live and love through him. I asked him if he had any praise or worship tapes to play in the car. He assured me that his wife had many. I told him to set his mind on the Lord Jesus, listen to some worship music, and go to work.

"See what happens; I believe Jesus can love through you," were my final words.

The next Sunday night, as I was setting up chairs in the parish hall for our prayer meeting, I looked down the hallway and saw Steve walking toward me. He was sporting a huge grin. He came up to me and gave me a big hug.

"What in the world happened to you?" I asked.

"You wouldn't believe what happened when I went to work that morning. I was loving people! I was looking at the people in my office through new eyes. It was amazing!"

The point is that Steve's life did not *change*. He is still a miserable, unloving, hateful wretch. The experiences of the past which had created his unloving character were not healed. But something new was added. He was not repaired; he was *replaced*. When Steve fails to walk in the Spirit and abide in Christ Jesus, the old, angry, unloving person will naturally surface again.

This reality, if it is not understood, often causes much confusion among Christians who have an experience with the Holy Spirit. The immediate result is what appears to be a changed life. They share their testimony, which says in effect, "I used to be this kind of person, but now, praise the Lord, I am a different person." But as time goes by, they discover that nothing has really changed. The old problems surface again. So rather than learning how to live and walk in the Spirit and abide in Christ, they seek a "new experience," thinking that they lost the old one.

NOT CHANGED BUT EXCHANGED

Human nature is molded by the experiences of life: It is possessed by pity, anger, bitterness, and worry; controlled by self-preservation; motivated by pride; threatened by rejection;

encouraged by success; driven by lust; and gripped by the fear of death. *Human nature cannot be changed*. For this reason, the challenge which confronts inner-healing teachers is an endless challenge.

This is the essential difference between what is offered in psychology and what is offered in Christianity. It is true that there are many life-changing experiences based upon psychological technique. I participated in an encounter group and experienced a dramatic change in my own life. People can attend a weekend *est* seminar, have someone scream profanities at them, come to the conclusion that they are responsible for their own ridiculous existence, get "it," and go home a changed person. Those who advocate Jungian psychology and venture into their own psyche are *changed* by the experience.

But the Christian life is not a *changed* life—it is an *exchanged* life. A Christian begins as a miserable, wretched sinner by nature, remains that way, and dies that way. Nothing ever changes. But the Christian is given an alternative life, *another life* to live in Christ Jesus. By living and walking in Christ Jesus, the Christian manifests new attitudes, new actions, new emotions, new thoughts, new desires. Yet his life is never changed. He is still a poor, miserable, wretched sinner *who has Jesus*! He is still a broken branch who has found a new *Vine*, an earthen vessel containing a new *treasure*, a miserable sinner holding on to the perfect life of Jesus Christ. Hallelujah!

Don't let anybody dig around in the depths of your alleged unconscious psyche and tell you what garbage is there, or what cause-and-effect relationship exists between the garbage in your psyche and the behavior of your life. You should know better than anyone else what garbage is a part of your human nature. That garbage is not going to be healed; it's finally going to be buried! But as far as life today is concerned, *for this you have Jesus*!

"Everybody needs inner healing!" is the claim of the inner-healing teachers. Of course they do! Everybody from Adam onward needs inner healing. All inner-healing teachers need inner healing. The whole world needs inner healing. Is that such a profound revelation? The human nature of every person born into this world is sick and needs inner healing. But there will never be an end to the ministry, nor can there be. Where do you stop? When does the digging cease? Will people arrive at the place where one day *they will no longer need inner healing*? Never!

Inner healing is not the answer to the sanctification question. JESUS IS! The apostle Paul declares: "He is the source of your life in Christ Jesus, whom God made our wisdom, our righteousness and sanctification and redemption" (1 Corinthians 1:30). Therefore, forgetting what is behind, press on to the mark of the high calling in Christ Jesus!

Notes

Notes

Chapter 1—An Intriguing Debate

1. Dave Hunt and T.A. McMahon, *The Seduction of Christianity* (Harvest House Publishers, 1985), pp. 211-25.
2. Ibid., p. 129.
3. Ibid., pp. 177-78.
4. Robert Wise et al, *The Church Divided* (Bridge Publishing, Inc., 1986), p. 39.
5. Viktor E. Frankl, *The Unconscious God* (Simon and Shuster, 1975), p. 75.

Chapter 2—The Key to Sanctification?

1. David Hazard, "An Inside Look at Inner Healing," in *Charisma*, Sep. 1986, p. 46.
2. Agnes Sanford, *The Healing Gifts of the Spirit* (Harper & Row, 1966), p. 116.
3. Ibid., p. 117.
4. Dr. Paul Yonggi Cho, *The Fourth Dimension*, Vol. 2 (Bridge Publishing, Inc., 1983), p. 52-53.
5. Sanford, *Healing Gifts*, p. 10.
6. Dennis and Rita Bennett, *Trinity of Man* (Logos International, 1979), pp. 137, 146.
7. John & Paula Sandford, *The Transformation of the Inner Man* (Bridge Publishing, Inc., 1982), p. 82.
8. Ruth Carter Stapleton, *The Gift of Inner Healing* (Bantam Books, Inc., 1976), p. xi.
9. Rita Bennett, *Emotionally Free* (Fleming H. Revell Co., 1982), p. 47.
10. John & Paula Sandford, *Transformation*, pp. 7, 8.
11. Dennis Bennett, "Another Wave of the Spirit?" in *Charisma*, Jan. 1985, p. 45.
12. Hazard in *Charisma*, Sep. 1986, p. 48.
13. Sandfords, *Transformation*, p. 4.
14. Paul Yonggi Cho, *The Fourth Dimension*, Vol. 1 (Logos International, 1979), p. 42.

Chapter 3—The Question of Biblical Authority

1. Wise et al, *Church Divided*, p. 42.
2. Richard Dortch, "Authors Twist Definition of Sorcery," in *Ministries*, Sep. 1986, p. 71.
3. Bernard Ramm, *Protestant Biblical Interpretation* (W. A. Wilde Company, 1956), pp. 122, 148-49.

Chapter 4—Freudian Understanding

1. Morton Kelsey, *Christianity As Psychology* (Augsburg Publishing House, 1986), p. 20.
2. The fifth edition of *Basic Psychology* by L. Dodge Fernald and Peter S. Fernald (Wm. C. Brown, 1985), p. 11, states regarding the relationship between psychology and evolution: "Darwin's *theory of evolution*, which states that any plant or animal species developed through modification of preexisting species, was highly controversial, but it had a tremendous effect on the study of human behavior and experience. It prompted all sorts of speculations about a continuity from the animal to the human mind and about the nature of animal mental life. Furthermore, the idea of animal instincts, which was well accepted, led to speculation about human instincts and to the study of human motivation."
3. Martin and Deidre Bobgan, *The Psychological Way/The Spiritual Way* (Bethany House Publishers, 1979), p. 49.
4. Sanford, *Healing Gifts*, pp. 140-41.
5. Bennetts, *Trinity*, p. 140.
6. Ibid., pp. 140-42.
7. For an excellent critique of Freudian theory see *The Psychological Way/The Spiritual Way* (Bethany, 1978) by Martin and Deidre Bobgan, pp. 68-75.
8. Philip Gold, "Psychoanalysis: Identity Crisis," in *Insight*, Dec. 1, 1986, pp. 8-13.
9. Laurence Miller, "In Search of the Unconscious," in *Psychology Today*, Dec. 1986, p. 60.
10. Viktor Frankl, *The Unconscious God* (Simon and Shuster, 1975), pp. 19-24.
11. Viktor Frankl, *The Unheard Cry for Meaning* (Simon and Shuster, 1978), p. 50.

12. Regarding dream causation, the Bobgans write: "At the present time, we neither know what dreams mean nor how they originate. Dream theories range from causation by instinctual drives to mere electro-chemical activity" (*The Psychological Way/The Spiritual Way*, p. 69).
13. Bennetts, *Trinity*, p. 138.
14. Jamie Buckingham, *Risky Living* (Logos International, 1976), p. 28.
15. "An Interview with Rita," from *The Morning Watch*, the newsletter of The Christian Renewal Association, Box 576, Edmonds, WA 98020. In her book *Emotionally Free* (Revell, 1982), Rita Bennett provides illustrations of this theory (pp. 136-37).
16. Frankl, *Unheard Cry*, p. 50.
17. Sigmund Freud, *Totem and Taboo* (Vintage Books, 1918), p. 190.
18. Stapleton, *Gift*, pp. 12-13.
19. W. Hugh Missildine, *Your Inner Child of the Past* (Simon and Shuster, 1963), p. 7.

Chapter 5—The Bridge to the Unconscious

1. Sanford, *Healing Gifts*, p. 118.
2. Bennett, *Emotionally Free*, pp. 74-89.
3. Sandfords, *Transformation*, p. 146.
4. Francis MacNutt, *The Prayer That Heals* (Ave Maria Press, 1981), p. 108.
5. Stapleton, *Inner Healing*, p. 23.
6. Wise et al, *Church Divided*, p. 84.
7. Bennett, *Emotionally Free*, p. 71.
8. Sigmund Freud, *The Ego and the Id* (W. W. Norton & Company, 1960), p. 11.
9. Mike and Nancy Samuels, *Seeing with the Mind's Eye* (Random House, 1975), p. 182.
10. Rudolf Otto, *The Idea of the Holy* (Oxford University Press, 1923), pp. 5-11.
11. William McGuire, *The Freud/Jung Letters* (Princeton University Press, 1974), p. 27.
12. C. G. Jung, *Memories, Dreams, Reflections* (Vintage Books, 1965), p. 150.
13. Joseph Campbell, *The Portable Jung* (Penguin Books, 1971), p. 39.
14. Mike and Nancy Samuels, *The Mind's Eye*, p. 182.
15. Aniela Jaffe, *C. G. Jung Word and Image* (Princeton University Press, 1979), pp. 115-16.
16. Carl G. Jung, *Man and His Symbols* (Doubleday, 1964), pp. 206-07.

17. Morton Kelsey, *Transcend* (Crossroad, 1985), p. 83.

Chapter 6—Is Jesus an Inner Spirit Guide?

1. "An Interview with Rita," in *The Morning Watch*, Dec. 1985.
2. Wise et al, *Church Divided*, pp. 84-87.
3. Ronald Shone, *Creative Visualization* (Thorsons, 1984), pp. 34-39.
4. Jose Silva, *The Silva Mind Control Method* (Pocket Books, 1978), p. 94.
5. William James, *The Varieties of Religious Experience* (Penguin Books, 1982), pp. 512-13.
6. Jung, *Memories*, p. 183.
7. Wise, *Church Divided*, pp. 84-85.
8. Peter Davids, "Is Christianity Being Seduced?" in *Charisma*, Mar. 1986, p. 33.
9. Harmon H. Bro, *Edgar Cayce On Religion and Psychic Experience* (Warner Books, 1970), p. 24, back cover.

Chapter 7—A Very Dangerous Journey

1. Wise et al, *Church Divided*, pp. 84-87.
2. Morton Kelsey, *The Other Side of Silence* (Paulist Press, 1976), p. 73.
3. Ibid., pp. 53-54, 140-41.
4. Mark Virkler, *Dialogue With God* (Bridge Publishing, 1986), p. 8.
5. Jung, *Memories*, pp. 180, 189-91.
6. Christopher F. Monte, *Beneath the Mask* (Holt, Rinehart and Winston, 1977, 1980), p. 276.
7. Morton Kelsey, *Resurrection* (Paulist Press, 1985), pp. 7-9.
8. Wallace Clift, *Jung and Christianity* (Crossroad, 1982), pp. 129-39.

Chapter 8—The Cult of the Unconscious

1. James, *Varieties*, pp. 511-13.
2. Calvin S. Hall, *A Primer of Freudian Psychology* (Mentor Books, 1954), p. 54.
3. Campbell, *Portable Jung*, p. 39.
4. Ted Dobson, *Inner Healing* (Paulist Press, 1978), p. 135.
5. Agnes Sanford, Taped teachings on "The Gifts of the Holy Spirit."
6. Cho, *Fourth*, Vol. 1., Foreword and pp. 41-43.
7. Norman Vincent Peale, *Positive Imaging* (Fleming H. Revell, 1982), p. 17.

8. Bennetts, *Trinity*, p. 140.
9. Dobson, *Inner Healing*, pp. 77-78, 111, 155.
10. Sanford, *Healing Gifts*, p. 10.
11. Hazard in *Charisma*, Sep. 1986, p. 49.

Chapter 9—God and the Unconscious

1. Dobson, *Inner Healing*, p. 155.
2. Sanford, *Healing Gifts*, p. 116.
3. Ibid., p. 136.
4. "Buckingham Report," Dec. 1985. Jamie Buckingham's newsletter to Christian leaders.
5. Richard J. Foster, *Celebration of Discipline* (Harper and Row, 1978), p. 137.
6. Ibid., p. 26.
7. Morton Kelsey, *Encounter With God* (Bethany Fellowship, Inc., 1972), p. 37.
8. Ibid., p. 109.
9. Ibid., p. 119.
10. John J. Heany, *Psyche and Spirit* (Paulist Press, 1984), pp. 199-209.
11. Hazard in *Charisma*, Sep. 1986, p. 49.
12. M. Scott Peck, *The Road Less Traveled* (Simon and Shuster, 1978), p. 282.
13. Ibid., p. 283.
14. Campbell, *Portable Jung*, p. 488.
15. Frankl, *Unconscious God*, p. 62.

Chapter 10—Altered Consciousness

1. Foster, *Celebration*, p. 17.
2. Jesse Penn-Lewis, *War on the Saints* (Thomas E. Lowe, Ltd., 1973), pp. 114-15, 151.
3. Sanders G. Laurie and Melvin K. Tucker, *Centering* (Destiny Books, 1978), p. 10.
4. Samuels, *Mind's Eye*, p. 273.
5. Lawrence LeShan, *How to Meditate* (Bantam Books, 1974), pp. 48-49.
6. Silva, *Mind Control*, p. 91.
7. Sanford, *Healing Gifts*, p. 137.
8. Bro, *Edgar Cayce*, p. 35.
9. Laurie and Tucker, *Centering*, pp. 164-65.
10. Howard M. Ervin, *This Which Ye See and Hear* (Logos International, 1972), p. 95.

11. Watchman Nee, *The Latent Power of the Soul* (Christian Fellowship Publishers, Inc., 1972), pp. 40-41.
12. Morton Kelsey, *Transcend* (Crossroad, 1985), pp. 2-12.
13. Virkler, *Dialogue*, pp. 6-7.
14. Edmond Jacobs, *Theology of the Old Testament* (Harper and Row, 1958), p. 241.

Chapter 11—Counterfeit Fruit

1. Jung, *Memories*, p. 143.
2. Davids in *Charisma*, Mar. 1986, p. 33.
3. James, *Varieties*, pp. 20-21.
4. Wise et all, *Divided*, p. 193.
5. James, *Varieties*, p. 21.
6. Ibid., p. 412.
7. Kelsey, *Other Side*, p. 53.
8. Carl Rogers, *Carl Rogers on Encounter Groups* (Harper and Row, 1970), p. 143.
9. M. Scott Peck, *What Return Can I Make?* (Simon and Shuster, 1985), p. 115.

Chapter 12—Back to Scripture

1. Wise, *Church Divided*, p. 38, Appendix A.
2. Jung, *Memories*, p. 210.
3. James, *Varieties*, p. 406.
4. Thomas Merton, *Mystics and Zen Masters* (Farrar, Straus and Giroux, 1961), p. 205.

ABOUT THE AUTHOR

The Rev. Donald G. Matzat is the pastor of Resurrection Lutheran (Missouri Synod) Church in Flushing, New York. Upon graduating from Concordia Seminary in St. Louis (M. Div.) in 1965, he served parishes in Southern Indiana and Michigan before moving back to his native New York City in 1979. Don has been involved in the charismatic movement since 1971 and has been a popular conference Bible teacher. In addition to having numerous articles published in magazines and renewal newsletters, Don edits his own publication, called "Bread of Life." He approaches the subject of inner healing from a background of solid biblical theology joined to charismatic experience.

Don and his wife, Dianne, have four children: Phil, Cindy, Susan, and Daniel.